THE MONEY HAT
and Other Hungarian Folk Tales

THE
MONEY HAT

and Other Hungarian Folk Tales

By

PEGGY HOFFMANN & GYURI BÍRÓ

Illustrated by GYURI BÍRÓ

THE WESTMINSTER PRESS

Philadelphia

STANDARD BOOK NO. 664–32458–4
LIBRARY OF CONGRESS CATALOG CARD NO. 79–85858

BOOK DESIGN BY
DOROTHY ALDEN SMITH

PUBLISHED BY THE WESTMINSTER PRESS ®
PHILADELPHIA, PENNSYLVANIA

PRINTED IN THE UNITED STATES OF AMERICA

S 1511517

To Eileen

CONTENTS

TOLD BY THREE VOICES . . .

THE SMALL COUNTRY of Hungary lies east of the Austrian Alps and north of the mountains of Yugoslavia in the very heart of South Central Europe. Divided by the Danube River, it is a historic land of plains and low mountains.

There these folk tales, centuries old, have been passed down for generations from grandfather to grandchildren on long winter evenings in front of a cozy fire. As in all folk literature, there are variations of detail from one storyteller to another, but the essential theme of each story is fairly consistent.

The reader is given many glimpses into traditional Hungarian life and thought. For instance, peasants, servants, and noblemen are always distinct classes, with no large middle class. The hero—or the victim, as the case may be—is always a man. When women do appear, they move in the background as witches, arrogant princesses, shrewish wives, and mistreated or misguided mothers. There is a certain amount of gentle irreverence for the church and the formalities of religion, although the good usually triumphs. Sometimes it is a precarious victory. Justice is swift and certain, and occasionally cruel, vicious, and uncompromising.

Some of the stories wander in and out of fantasy, others reflect reality. Several have real settings at places that still exist and can be seen if one visits Hungary. In all of them we can recognize a bit of ourselves—not always in a flattering light. Children have always enjoyed acting out many of the stories as small dramas.

Gyuri Bíró, who was born in Budapest in 1942, heard these stories and many like them from his grandfather in his earliest childhood. He translated them in his mind from Hungarian to German, telling them to his wife in German. She in turn translated them from German to English and told them into a tape recorder, sending the tapes to me. I then wrote them for publication. If I have put the tales into readable and interesting form, it is because the heart of each story is real and appealing.

PEGGY HOFFMANN

THE MONEY HAT

Now I will tell you a story of three students, great strong fellows with beards, who decided to go out into the world to make their own way. They set off on a bright summer morning and were soon in the open country. After a while they came to a small village and saw an old peasant trudging along the street.

"Hello, Uncle!" one of the students called to him. "Pray tell us, how long will the world last?"

The peasant raised his hat respectfully and answered, "One day less than today."

The young fellows roared with laughter. The second one asked him, "On what tree does Morality grow?"

Again he replied politely. "Even among weeds," he told them, "there can be beautiful flowers."

"A clever answer! A very clever answer!" the three agreed. "Let's ask him one more."

"My turn," said the third. "Pray tell us, what is under your hat?" he asked. "It must be something valuable because you always put the hat back on your head so quickly and so carefully."

The old man bowed again. "Let the young gentlemen follow me into this Gasthaus and I will show them."

The three students held back. They did not have one forint among them, not one. How could they go into an inn when they had no money?

"He invited us, didn't he?" they asked each other. "Let's try it."

The peasant was standing patiently at the door of the Gasthaus, waiting for them to make up their minds. When he saw that they had decided to follow him, he whispered to the innkeeper that they were to be served wine until the bill amounted to five forint.

The three sat down at a table and began to drink, smacking their lips. "This is the way to live!" they declared. "Come into a Gasthaus with no money, sit down at a table, and drink fine wines! Such very fine wines!" They pounded on the table for more service.

The innkeeper came to them and said, "You owe me five forint, my good men. I cannot possibly bring you anything more until you pay me."

"But we haven't any money!" they said, becoming worried. "Look at our pockets. Completely empty!" All three of them turned their pockets inside out. Not

one fillér did they have, not the tiniest fraction of a cent. The innkeeper began to frown and to tap his foot.

The peasant watched with a smile, then he said to the innkeeper, "My hat will pay you." He took off his hat and shook it. A shining new coin fell to the floor. He picked up the money and handed it to the owner of the Gasthaus. Then he turned to the three students. "Now you see what is under my hat," he told them, with another bow.

The students were dumbfounded. They thought— if only the hat could belong to them instead of to that old man! What great and important personages they could be if they just owned that hat! They would only have to shake it and they would hear the clink of money falling to the floor! They must have the hat. They must!

However, the peasant refused to sell the hat! The students talked earnestly with each other and vowed that no matter how much it cost, they must have the hat. They would find the money to pay for it in some way. Perhaps they could even make the hat pay for itself. Again they begged the old man to sell it to them.

"You don't have any money," he reminded them. "You just showed me that your pockets are absolutely empty. How can you buy my hat? Or anything else, for that matter? You couldn't even pay for your wines."

"We'll get the money!" they said stubbornly. "We promise you. Somehow or other we will find a way to pay you. We simply must have that hat!"

Finally the peasant gave in. "I'm an old man any-way," he said with a sigh. "If you can pay me five hundred forint for my remarkable hat, you can have it. It's a sacrifice, but my wife and I ought to be able to live on five hundred forint until we die. Here," he said sadly, "take it."

"Oh, thank you, thank you!" they cried as all three of them reached for the hat at once. Then they began whispering anxiously to each other. "But where can we get the money? We have to think fast. Where?"

"The Count!" one of them said. "The man who is head of this village. He'll lend it to us, I'm sure. We look honest. And anyway, once we have the hat, we can repay him in no time."

The three students hurried off to find the Count and tell him their story. How he really felt about the matter is neither here nor there, but at any rate he did agree to let them have the money. They rushed back with the five hundred forint to the waiting peasant and were soon on their way with the hat, laughing and singing for joy.

Whatever they wanted would be paid for by the hat! Shake it and, presto! a coin would fall out. Shake it again, another coin! Or possibly several, all at once.

At the next village the three students rushed into an inn and ordered a huge dinner. "Everything you have!" they told the waiter grandly. "Bring us your finest food. We must have the best, and plenty of it!"

They ate and ate and ate, hardly stopping for breath. It was a delicious meal. They kept the hat in the center of the table where they could admire it. Our-friend-the-hat, they called it. "The hat will pay," they told themselves happily. "A very special hat it is! The hat that spits money! Oh, beautiful, wonderful, generous hat! Waiter, more of everything! At once!"

When they finished their meal the three were almost too stuffed to get up from the table. The bill for the food was enormous, but they reached confidently for their-friend-the-hat. It would pay. Ah, beautiful hat!

They shook it. And shook it. And shook it! They turned the hat bottom side up and inside out. They thumped it and pounded it and squeezed it. Nothing came out.

The hat was not going to produce any money to pay for their dinner, their delicious, expensive dinner. The waiter glared at them and went off to find the owner. The owner also glared at them. Then he yelled at them and motioned them toward the kitchen. They would have to work until every single bite was paid for.

It took a long time.

"We'll get even with that peasant," the three students said fiercely. "We'll get even if it's the last thing we ever do. Come on, let's go back to that village where we first met him."

On their way they came to a large forest, and, as luck would have it, the peasant was working there,

chopping down trees. He recognized them as soon as he saw them, but it was too late to try to escape. He knew that he would have to think fast to keep them from knowing who he was. Quickly he picked up a saw that was near him and began sawing furiously at a large tree trunk. "Help!" he cried. "Help! This big tree is going to fall on me and crush me! Help!"

He pressed his shoulder heavily against the tree trunk so the students would think he was actually keeping it from toppling over. Hearing his cries for help, the three came running to him.

The old man kept turning his face away from them, all the time shouting, "Help! Oh, the dear God in Heaven must have sent you fine young gentlemen to save me. You must have known there was a treasure buried under this tree." He kept grunting and pushing, puffing as if the task were too great for him. "I was going to dig out the treasure myself as soon as I got this big old tree out of the way," he said, gasping for breath, "but my saw cut was too low. If I move away now, the tree will fall on me and crush me. Oh, the dear God must have sent you."

He sounded so frightened that the three young travelers rushed to his aid. "Here," he said when they came up to him, "let me show you where to stand so you can hold up the tree while I go for help. I'll get a stout rope and tie it to the strongest limb, on the very top of the tree, then we can pull it so the tree falls toward the west. The treasure is under the east side, as I'm sure you know, so we must make sure that the tree falls in the opposite direction. Oh, I am so glad you came! Here, sir, you stand right here. And, you, over there. Now push! Hard! Harder! Ah, that ought to do it." He straightened up as if the weight of the tree had almost broken his back. "I'll run as fast as I can to the village and come right back with a good rope. It won't take but a few minutes."

He ran off toward the village while the three students held up the tree. They waited all morning, all afternoon, and all evening, afraid that the tree would fall on them if they dared to move. Finally the first student said crossly, "We can't stay here forever!"

"I'm tired and I'm hungry," said the second one, who was always tired and hungry. "And I don't think that old man is ever going to come back with a rope."

"He isn't coming back at all," said the third, who sometimes had more sense than the other two. "I have an idea. Let's all spring away from the tree at once, as far and as fast as we can. I'll count. Are you ready?" He took a deep breath. "One! Two! Three! *Now!*" They all jumped away from the tree. Nothing happened. The tree stood as straight and strong and thick as ever. The saw cuts that the peasant said he had made were only a half-inch deep.

"That terrible old man has made fools of us!" said the first student.

"Again!" said the second one.

"For the last time!" roared the third. "Let's go into

that village and find him. He'll be sorry he ever laid eyes on us. And he'll never forget us, believe me!" The student made great fists of his hands and flexed the muscles of his arms, even though they ached from holding up the tree. "We'll show him!"

"Let's eat first," said the second student. "Then we can show him."

While they were getting angrier and angrier and angrier, the poor peasant was beginning to worry. He couldn't find any place to hide. He kept asking his wife to find him, wherever he hid himself, and she always found him. He hid in the cupboard, under the bed, behind the door, back of the stove, up in the straw-stack, on the roof, out in the cowshed, and high up in the apple tree, but still she found him. He was getting desperate.

At last his wife, who was getting desperate too, said to him, "Listen, my husband, don't keep trying to hide. It's much better that you pretend you are dead. Lie down here. I'll cover you with this sheet. When they come and see that you are dead, they'll go away again and that will be the end of it."

"It's worth a try," said her husband. "I hope we can manage to fool them. We must! Bring the sheet. Quick!"

The moment she got him covered with the sheet, she heard a knock at the door, a loud angry knock. Covering her face with her apron, she began to cry. "Oh, my good husband," she sobbed. "My sweet, kind

husband! Why did he have to die? Why, oh, why?" she wailed, all the time watching the young men from between her fingers.

The three stepped inside. "Why are you crying, old woman?" they asked.

"Why shouldn't I cry?" she asked in turn. "My good husband is lying here dead, and I am left all alone in the world, a poor widow with no one to take care of me."

"Say," one of them whistled, "I think I know this man. He was a great big crook! A crook!" The student reached for a heavy stick that was lying near the door. *Whack!* He hit the peasant with all his might. "Here, you old thief! You big liar!" *Whack!* He hit him again. "Take this!"

"Y-e-e-e-e-e-e-e-e-e-ow!" screeched the peasant, leaping up in pain, and of course still very much alive. Keeping his wits about him nevertheless, he knelt in front of his visitors. "Oh, you wonderful, kind, thoughtful young gentlemen!" he said thankfully. "God shall surely bless you. Now I know for certain that this stick has miraculous powers. Yesterday in my garden I saw a dead dog. I picked up this stick and hit him with it. Immediately the dog sprang up and ran away! Just like that!" He snapped his fingers. "He ran away!"

"He did?"

"Like that?"

"Dead, you said?"

24

All three of the students were talking at once.

"Did what? Oh, yes, I forgot. He ran away. That's what he did. Just like that!" The peasant snapped his fingers again. "Then I thought to myself, That can't be. This old stick can't possibly be magic. Maybe that dog wasn't dead at all, just sleeping."

He saw that they were listening to every word, so he went on, watching to make sure he didn't get whacked again. "Then my neighbor told me that the Count's favorite horse had just died, and the Count was very sad because he loved that horse." The old man wiped away a tear. "So, right away, I went over there and, without telling the Count what I was going to do, I hit his horse with my magic stick. Of course you know what happened!"

"What happened?" asked the second student, entranced.

"The horse jumped up and began dancing and prancing all around the courtyard, and the Count wept for joy. His beautiful horse was alive, all because of my magic stick."

"A miracle!" said the three students. "Truly a miracle!"

Feeling that he was safe, the peasant got to his feet and said to his wife, "My dear, why don't we give these fine young fellows all that money the Count gave me for saving his horse? We have so much more than we can ever use. And we can live by this stick. Whenever some great and important gentleman dies, I shall hurry to him with my stick and bring him instantly back to life. We shall be rich because of this stick!"

"Ha!" said the young men. "You have already fooled us twice, and that's enough. We are going to take that magic stick away from you, you old crook. You can keep your money."

"No! No!" he protested. "I must keep my stick. I will give you all the money you can carry. And more. I will fill your pockets with gold. You will be millionaires! Only leave me my precious treasure, my stick."

Now you must remember that there were three students—great big strong fellows, young ones. And only one peasant—an old one at that, and small. And, of course, his wife—a weak, helpless woman. In no time at all those big brutes had overpowered the two and had stolen the magic stick. They went running off as fast as they could.

The peasant was doubled up with laughter. "Just let them take that old stick!" he crowed. "They can have it. I've fooled them again. Three times now I've fooled them."

Carrying the stick as if it were made of diamonds, the three big strong students went on their journey, over mountains and valleys and far across the land, until one day they came to a town where there was a funeral procession in the street. Six fine horses, their heads decorated with black feathers, were pulling a shiny black coach carrying a richly decorated coffin.

"Who has died?" they asked.

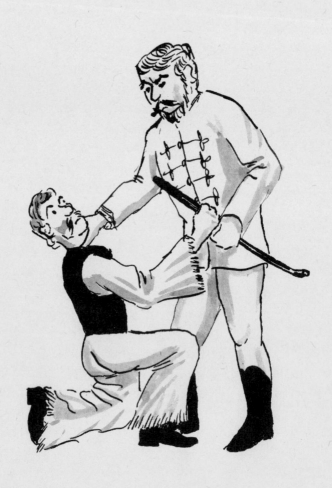

"The young Countess," said a man sadly. "The beautiful young daughter of the Count. In the next carriage are her parents and her sorrowing sweetheart, the Crown Prince. Oh, it is so sad."

"Our stick! Our magic stick can bring her back to life!" They hurried to the coach where they could see the Countess's mother by a window. "Madam!" they said. "If you will allow us, we can bring your daughter back to life! All we need to do is to see her. We will touch her once with our magic stick, and she will live again! We promise you."

The poor heartbroken mother nodded her consent and gave the driver a signal to stop. The oldest student, who was sometimes the smartest, stepped to the body of the young Countess and struck her neck a sharp blow with the heavy stick. The townspeople watched him with horror. What a terrible thing to do! But even as they stared, the Countess gasped, sat up, rubbed her eyes and began to smile.

"A miracle!" everyone exclaimed. "Truly a miracle. She lives!"

There were balls and feasts and celebrations all over the land, and each of the three young men who had saved the Countess was given a huge sack of gold and as much food and drink as he could hold. They had new clothes, fine horses to ride, anything they wished for.

Since they were honest young men—if a little gullible at times—they went back to the Count in the village and paid him the five hundred forint he had lent them. Then, since they were so rich from all the gold they had been given, they never had to use the stick again.

And a lucky thing it was! Because, of course, there was no magic in the stick. The young Countess had choked on a fish bone, and the sharp blow on her neck had forced it out, so that she could breathe again.

Well, that's the way it was. This is the end of the story. Every word of it is true.

FERENC PATÓCSY

PATÓCSY the nobleman was so rich that he owned seventeen villages as well as a huge and beautiful castle called Szadvar. He was also a very religious man. He had given a group of monks a fine piece of land, had built them a comfortable monastery, and had always paid all their living expenses. The monks were grateful for the many things he had done for them, but, being human, they kept a close watch for other favors that might come their way.

Patócsy had one son, named Ferenc. The monks had watched the boy grow up, almost from the moment of his birth. The head monk, the Abbot, had officiated at the joyous ceremonies when the boy was christened. The greatest dream of the Abbot and the monks was that the child might study to become a priest. They figured that if he did, the monastery— and they themselves, of course—would possess not only the land and buildings where they lived, and the expenses of their food and clothing, but also the great castle Szadvar and the seventeen villages surrounding it. They spent a great deal of time trying to convince the nobleman that it would be a fine service to the Lord if the boy, Ferenc, became interested in theology and devoted his life to religion.

Patócsy told them time after time, "My son must make up his own mind as to what he wants to do in the world. It's his life, and he has the right to choose for himself the way he will spend it."

"Of course! Exactly! To be sure! An admirable policy!" the monks told him. "But the best possible life is the religious life!"

"A man can be religious without becoming a priest or a monk," the nobleman reminded them, annoyed with their pestering. "Look at me! I am one of the most religious men in all of Hungary, yet I am not a cloistered monk, shutting myself away from the world. I have married and have a son, I have traveled widely, and I live very much in the life of the people around me. Yet I am religious. Very much so. Now please stop bothering me about my son. For the last time, I am telling you that Ferenc will decide for himself."

With this sharp rebuke the nobleman considered the matter closed, but the monks did not. They were biding their time and watching everything that happened. Not even the smallest incident escaped their notice.

When Ferenc came of age, he had a long talk with his father and told him that he had made up his mind. Ferenc would become a chemist. He had no interest in becoming a priest or in going into a monastery.

In no time at all the Abbot and his monks learned of the conversation. They hurried to the castle and requested that Patócsy not forget them in his will. They were greatly worried—Ferenc might turn them out of their comfortable quarters and take away the bounty that gave them such an easy life that they never lifted a finger to do any physical labor. They went to the castle so often and were so insistent that the nobleman finally called in a lawyer and asked him to draw up a last will and testament. This is the way it read:

Upon my death, my property shall be divided into two parts. One part shall be my castle, Szadvar, and all its furnishings, all the animals and tools on its farmlands and all of the seventeen villages which surround it. The second part shall consist of a strip of land at the edge of the forest, and the hunting lodge which is situated on it. My son, Ferenc, is to receive whichever part of the legacy pleases the monks who live in the monastery adjacent to my property.

He gave the monks a copy of the last will and testament and told them to go away and leave him alone. They were delighted with his plans. Soon afterward the nobleman died. The property was divided into the two parts that the will had specified. The monks, nat-

urally, laid claim to the first part, the castle, the tools, the animals, and the seventeen villages.

It was obvious that the second part was not much of an inheritance. The hunting lodge was little more than a one-room shack, with no heat, and only a brambled footpath leading to it. The strip of land was about forty feet wide and sixty feet long, choked with vines and weeds, and overrun with snakes. When he went to look at it, Ferenc was heartsick. Since he had grown up at Szadvar and was an only child, he had always assumed that the castle would be his home for the rest of his life. But his father's will had directed that he should get whichever part of the legacy pleased the monks—and it had surely pleased them to give him the lesser share.

The monks, on the other hand, were ecstatic with their legacy. They immediately took possession of the beautiful castle and all its furnishings and animals and tools and the vast income from the surrounding villages. Enraged with their selfishness, Ferenc went to see them.

"Are you trying to punish me," he asked them angrily, "for not going into the priesthood? My father always told me that I should make up my own mind about my life. You know that. I decided—with his consent, I might remind you—that I am to be a chemist. I want to do something good for the people of the world."

"A most praiseworthy ambition!" they assured him.

"Szadvar has always been my home!" Ferenc continued stubbornly. "Always! Why do you persist in treating me so harshly by turning me out of my own home and making me try to exist in that dilapidated old shack?"

"We are only carrying out your sainted father's wishes," they told him piously. "The law is the law, you know. We'd be the very last persons on earth to break the law. We are doing exactly as your father instructed in his last will and testament."

"I know what he wanted for me," Ferenc persisted.

He set out to consult a judge, carrying a copy of his father's last will and testament with him. He went from one judge to another, but each man told him that his father's wishes were being fulfilled just as the document stated. The Abbot and the monks were entirely within their rights.

Ferenc finally went to the King, who was celebrated everywhere for his fairness and was known far and wide as Matthias the Just. The King listened carefully to his story, asking questions and making sure that he had all the facts. Then he sent word to the Abbot that he and his monks were to come to the palace for a conference.

"Now, gentlemen," he said to them when they had arrived, "let me hear your side of this argument. I want to know all the details."

"Your Majesty," said the Abbot, putting on a show of being humble, "you know how poor the church is and under what great need our monasteries are. You also know, Your Majesty, that a young man of Ferenc's talents and good qualities can always make his own way in the world. He does not need his father's great wealth, but we do."

"Is this the true issue?" asked the King judiciously. "Your need for the nobleman Patócsy's great wealth? Or is the issue the true interpretation of his wishes as he expressed them in his last will and testament?"

"Both!" Several of the monks spoke at once. "We want the castle and all its furnishings and its animals and the seventeen villages surrounding it. And our great benefactor, the father of this selfish young man, wanted us to have them. In his great wisdom and generosity he wrote this will—"

"I have a copy right here," the King interrupted them. "I see that it indicates that his only son, Ferenc, is to receive whatever pleases the residents of the monastery which is adjacent to his property. That refers to you, of course?"

"Yes, yes! Of course! We're the ones!" There was a happy chorus of answers. "He was always a very religious man."

The King looked at the men as if he could see into their hearts, his eyes bright and wise. "Does the castle and all its wealth please you? Do you like it?"

"Oh, yes, Your Majesty! We are delighted with it! We are overjoyed!"

The King turned to Ferenc. "My congratulations,

noble sir!" he said graciously. "The estate is yours!"

Astounded, the monks gasped and started complaining. The King silenced them. "You will recall," he said to Ferenc, "that your father's last will and testament specified that you were to receive whatever portion of the estate pleased the monks."

"Yes, Your Majesty," said Ferenc, puzzled.

"As you and I can see, and as these gentlemen have so clearly and enthusiastically stated," the King went on, "the castle and its riches please them very much. Is that not so?"

"Yes, very much," said Ferenc.

"Very, very much!" said the monks in unison.

"Then it is yours, my son. The law completely spells it out," said King Matthias the Just. "You are to have the portion that pleases them. The matter is settled."

"But—but—" sputtered the Abbot.

"That can't be—" grumbled the monks.

"The hearing is over!" said the King sternly. "Perhaps if you had not been quite so greedy, the will might have been written differently." He turned to Ferenc with a smile. "Young man, I wish you a long and useful life. I congratulate you for wanting to be a chemist, and I hope you will do some good in the world with your knowledge. Go in peace, Patócsy the nobleman. Go in peace."

Which he did.

LAZY GYURKA

ONCE there was a poor widow who had three sons. The oldest was a shoemaker and the second a tailor. Both of them worked hard, but the youngest one, Gyurka, was very lazy. He got up at noon, ate everything he could find, and spent the rest of the day either taking a nap or wandering around the village square talking to anyone who would listen. He let his mother chop wood, build fires, tend the geese, the cow, and the pig, grow the vegetables and the fruit, wash and iron all their clothes, and keep the cottage clean. Gyurka wouldn't even move his big feet so that she could sweep under them.

Finally his hardworking brothers lost their tempers. "That Gyurka is a big loafer!" they said. "He's healthy and strong and *lazy!* Let's tell that worthless good-for-nothing that he has to go to work, or else!"

So they did.

A week later Gyurka set out for the city to become an apprentice and learn a trade. His mother packed him a big lunch and brushed his clothes so he would make a good impression on anyone who might want to hire him. His brothers watched him until he was out of sight, making sure that he actually went and didn't stop in town to waste his time.

Alas, Gyurka didn't like to work. Not as a pot maker, because he got so dirty. Not as a tailor, because the needles stabbed his fingers. Not as an ironmonger, because heavy things fell on his toes. Not as a cook, because the pepper made him sneeze. Not as a stable-man, because the horses nipped at him. Not as a policeman, because he forgot to watch for robbers. Not as a postman, because he read all the letters and people complained. Not as an apothecary, because he couldn't tell pounds from ounces or pints from quarts. He had as many as three jobs in one day, but he always found excuses to get out of all of them.

Finally Gyurka sent word to his mother that she must come and get him. He didn't like the city, and there was no job that suited him.

So she came.

They were a sad pair, walking along the road to their village, the poor widow weeping and her big husky son staying far behind, pretending he wasn't with her. Then they saw a man with a red beard and leaning on a cane coming down the road toward them.

42

"What is wrong?" he asked Gyurka's mother sympathetically. "You are crying as if your heart would break, and this great strong fellow stays at a distance. What is the trouble?"

She began telling him her story, sobbing as she asked hopelessly what the future could possibly bring.

"Don't worry any more," the man told her. "It happens that I need a manservant—you can see how badly I limp—and this young son of yours will be just right. The work is easy, and on top of that I'll pay him ten times the usual salary."

"How am I to know that what you say is true?" she asked him tearfully. "I have never seen you before."

"Just trust me, madam," the man said with a big smile. "I will need your son for only one short year. Please be here at this spot and at this same hour, twelve months from today, and you shall have him back. I promise you on my word of honor."

While the worried woman was trying to decide what to do, both Gyurka and the red-bearded man disappeared, right before her eyes. There was no sign of either of them anywhere.

When she got home her older sons said carelessly, "So the lazy oaf is gone. So what? You'll have him back at the end of the year. And he'll have lots of money. Even if he doesn't, you won't miss it, because he has never earned any. What else can you do but wait?"

The months passed. On the appointed day and hour, Gyurka's mother was at the appointed spot, waiting. And waiting. And waiting. Neither her son nor the lame man came near. And still she waited.

Toward evening a white-whiskered old fellow hobbled up and asked her what she was doing there, so she told him the whole story.

"Did the man have a red beard?" he asked her.

"Yes. A red beard."

"And did he limp and carry a heavy cane?"

"Yes! That's the man!" she answered eagerly. "Do you know him?"

"I'm afraid I do, my good woman. Or at least I know who he is. Your son, I'm sorry to say, has been carried off by the Devil. There is little hope that you will ever see Gyurka again."

"Oh, no!" she wailed. "That can't be true!"

The old man patted her on the shoulder. "You are fortunate," he told her gently. "I am the great magician known as Abracadabra. I may be able to help you. However, my powers are not nearly as strong as the Devil's—"

"Anything you can do for me—anything—" the woman begged.

"Here is my little rabbit," he told her, "and here is an unopened rosebud. The rabbit will lead you straight to the gates of Hell—I'm sure you could never find the way there by yourself. The rosebud will burst into full bloom when you are directly in front of your son, so that you will know him no matter what disguise the Devil has put on him."

45

"A loving mother would recognize her own son anywhere!" she protested.

"Maybe," the magician said with a mysterious smile. "But you'd better take the rosebud, just in case. The Devil is extremely clever."

Before she could thank him or ask any questions, the old man disappeared in a puff of smoke, so she started following the little rabbit as he hopped away. The journey was a long one, over mountains and plains and through deep valleys and dark forests, but at last she saw a shining red gate gleaming in the distance.

At once the rabbit disappeared—just as the old man had—in a puff of smoke. Since the gate was not locked she went through it and began to look around. She found herself in a large room, elegantly furnished in rich red velvet and satin. At the far end, near a glowing fireplace, was an ornate throne sparkling with rubies. On it sat the Devil himself, haughty and stern, dressed in crimson silk.

"What do you want, old woman?" he growled at her, his eyes glittering.

"You did not keep your share of our bargain," she said bravely. "The year is over. Where is my son? And where is all the money you promised him, on your word of honor?"

"My *word of honor?*" he scoffed. "Never mind, you'll get your boy. Just pick him out and take him away." He blew a shrill whistle. The room was sud-

denly swarming with all kinds of hideous creatures, big and little, fat and thin. The Devil was astonished when the woman went up to one of them and said simply, "This is my son."

The Devil was furious. He leaped from his throne and with his wicked sword chopped all the creatures into thousands of small pieces, put them into a vat-sized kettle and mashed them into a pulp. The Devil can do things like that in a split second with no trouble at all.

He poured out the pulp and skillfully shaped it into new creatures, the same number as before, but all exactly alike. "Now find him!" he sneered at her.

Frightened, but determined to outwit the Devil, Gyurka's mother took the rosebud and walked around the room among the dozens of identical beings. "Here he is," she said happily, as the rosebud opened to full bloom. "This one is Gyurka, my son."

The Devil was even angrier than before, if that was possible. Gyurka was the kind of fellow he always liked. He had become very fond of the lad. "You have found him," he snarled, "but I will not let him go!"

"Oh, yes, you are!" said Gyurka, who had discovered that he didn't like the work there either. In an instant he had turned a somersault and changed himself into a bird. Away he flew, high in the sky. But the Devil would never give up so easily. He also turned a big somersault, made himself into a powerful hawk and flew off in hot pursuit after Gyurka.

There was nothing for the poor widow to do but to make her way home, sad and discouraged. She knew that her older sons wouldn't care whether she found the youngest one or not, so she went about her work, saying nothing.

As for Gyurka, he was so happy to be free that he flew straight for home. When he was almost there, he heard a hawk overtaking him and knew that it was the Devil. Far below him he saw a crowd of young people dancing in a green meadow. He darted down out of the sky and turned himself into a bright-colored scarf. Just as quickly the hawk changed himself into a handsome and charming young man.

One of the girls reached for the scarf and put it around her neck. The handsome young man asked her to be his partner for the next dance, although he was a stranger to her. Off they whirled, in time to the gay music. Then the handsome young man tried to pull the scarf away from her. The girl screamed for help.

Immediately all the young men fell on the stranger and began beating him unmercifully. "What are you doing to this girl?" they shouted at him. "Who are you? Where did you come from? Don't you have any manners? How could you treat a girl so rudely?" They kept on beating him until his whole body was a mass of bruises.

The Devil felt terrible. He had never been treated so badly. He wanted only one thing—to escape from these big brutes and get back to good old safe Hell, where he was the king. He never wanted to see or hear of Gyurka again. Never.

Seeing that the Devil was so busy defending himself, Gyurka did a quick flip-flop and became a bird

again, skimming off toward home. Even his brothers
were glad to see him. They began to ask all manner of
questions about what he had learned and what it was
like in Hell.

"Forget it," Gyurka said crossly. "I'm tired. Go
away. I need sleep."

In the morning they asked him again. "You must
have learned some kind of trade there," the brothers
persisted. "People always say that the Devil finds work
for idle hands. We don't care what it was, but if you
can do something to bring in some money, please get
at it."

Gyurka sat up, yawning and stretching. "No problem," he told them grandly. "Close your eyes and count to three. When you open them you will see a beautiful horse standing in front of you. Take him to the market and sell him for the highest price you can get. It's very simple."

While they had their eyes closed and were counting to three, Gyurka somersaulted out of bed and turned himself into a magnificent black stallion, pawing at the ground outside their door. Delighted, the brothers led the horse to market and sold him for a great amount of money. The fat rich man who bought him put him in a stable with other expensive animals and forgot all about him. Gyurka waited three days, then early one morning he somersaulted out of his stall, became a bird, and flew home.

Again he became a fine horse and his brothers sold him at the market. Their mother was overjoyed at their increasing wealth, and his brothers soon forgave him for the many years he had been so worthless. They paid no attention to the bitter complaints of the men who had bought the beautiful horse, only to have it disappear the next day or so.

"How should we know where the animal is?" they would ask piously. "We saw you leading it away from the market, and that was the end of it."

There came a day when the man who bought him was an old, hardworking peasant, who counted out the forint to pay for the stallion from a thin, worn purse tied inside his belt. As soon as he got the horse home, the peasant hitched him to a heavy plow and set him to work in a huge field.

From the first light of morning until far into the night, the poor horse pulled the plow, almost falling into his stall from exhaustion, too tired to somersault. If he couldn't somersault, he couldn't turn himself into a bird to fly home. Gyurka's brothers had become so rich that they forgot all about him and never bothered to hunt for him.

So, because he had cheated so many people and had never done a moment of honest toil, Gyurka remained a horse for the rest of his life, working from dawn to darkness, winter and summer, seven days a week, year in and year out.

When he died, only the peasant missed him.

THE FOX
AND
THE WOODCUTTER

ONCE there was a simple peasant whose job it was to cut wood in the forest. One day when he had finished his work and was going through a clearing on his way home, he saw a strange sight ahead of him. Two animals were fighting, right in the middle of the path.

When they separated for a moment he saw that one was a bear and the other was a rabbit. Imagine a bear fighting a rabbit! The man thought it was the funniest thing he had ever seen. He burst out laughing.

The bear heard him. Suddenly he tossed the rabbit to the ground and lumbered over to the woodcutter. "Gr-r-r-r-r!" he gr-r-r-r-ed. "If there is anything on earth that I can't stand, it is to have someone laugh at me. *Gr-r-r-r-r-r-r!*"

"S-sorry!" gasped the terrified fellow.

"Do you know what I'm going to do?" The bear's

hot breath was right in his face. "I'm going to eat you! That ought to teach you a lesson. And I'm hungry. You look as if you would make a tasty meal. Gr-r-r-r!"

The woodcutter fell on his knees. "Oh, please let me go home first to say good-by to my family," he begged. "They'll worry about me if I don't."

"Well, I suppose I could do that," said the bear, who was either stupid or softhearted. "But remember," and he shook his paw under the man's nose, "you are to be here at this very spot at sunrise. Not a moment later!"

"I won't forget!" the woodcutter promised. "I'll be right here at sunrise tomorrow!" He ran away from the bear as fast as his legs would carry him.

When he was safely out of sight, the peasant leaned against a tree to get his breath. While he was resting a fox came along the path.

"What's the matter with you?" the fox asked him. "You look as if you had seen a ghost!"

"It's worse than that," the man gulped as he told the fox what had happened to him. "And that bear will be waiting for me."

"A bear, eh? My old enemy," said the fox. "Well, don't lose your head. If we use our brains, there's nothing to be afraid of. Do you have a big sack at your house?"

"Yes, I guess so," said the man.

"When you come back here tomorrow morning," said the fox, "you must bring the biggest sack you can find. And an ax, a good strong one."

"A sack and an ax," the woodcutter repeated. "What are we going to do with them?"

"I shall hide in the bushes," the fox told him. "When you come to meet the bear and he starts after you, I'll blow my hunting horn. *Ta-ran-ta-ra! Ta-ran-ta-ra!* Bears are afraid of hunters, you know. So when he hears the horn, he'll ask you if there are any hunters around here."

"Yes! Yes! And what do I tell him?"

"You say that you saw a whole crowd of hunters heading this way with their guns loaded, looking for bears. That will scare him, so then you tell him you can help him escape. He can hide in your big sack until the hunters have gone away."

"Excellent!" said the man. "Then what?"

"This is where using your brains comes in," the fox told him modestly. "I'll come along and I'll say to you, 'What do you have in that sack, my good man?' and you'll say, 'Nothing but some old logs for my fireplace,' and you'll take your ax and give the sack a great big whack! Make sure you hit the bear right on the head, and hit him hard. You must finish him off with that first blow, or it will be too bad for you!"

"I know," said the woodcutter. "But my arms are strong from all the years I have worked in the forest. *Whack!* One blow! That's the way I'll do it." He pretended to take a powerful swing with his ax. "I am most grateful to you. However, I know you would not do me this great favor without some kind of reward. What do you want from me in return?" he asked.

"Very little, really," the fox answered. "Seven hens and a rooster would be plenty. Nice fat ones, of course. Young and healthy."

"Seven hens and a rooster?" The poor man knew that he did not have them, but if that was what the fox wanted for saving his life, he would have to find them somehow. He went on home and found a large sack and an ax, not telling his family what he was going to do with them, and not telling them, either, that he would have to find seven hens and a rooster.

Very early in the morning, as he had promised, he slipped out the door and went to the appointed place in the forest. Sure enough, the bear was waiting, licking his lips.

"Come here!" he ordered the frightened woodcutter. "I am very hungry. Starving, if you want the truth. It's been a long time since I had a decent meal. Come over here. There's no reason for you to be afraid of me. Ah-h-h!"

The bear's sharp white teeth and his red jaws and tongue were only inches from the man's head.

Just then there rang out the loud clear sound of a hunter's horn. *Ta-ran-ta-ra! Ta-ran-ta-ra!* The bear's jaws snapped shut in surprise as the woodcutter leaped out of the way.

"Are there any hunters around here?" the bear asked fearfully, his breath whistling between his teeth.

"That sounded exactly like a hunting horn!"

"Yes, there are," the man told him. "I saw a whole group of them as I was coming here for our appointment. They had their guns loaded and they were looking for bears."

"What am I going to do?" asked the bear, quivering with terror.

"I suppose I could let you hide in my big sack," said the woodcutter. "It is probably large enough, and they wouldn't dream of looking for you there, if you stay very quiet."

"Oh, I will, I will," the bear promised, climbing frantically into the open end of the sack. The man pulled it tight shut. "You are so kind," the bear mumbled as he curled up inside, hardly breathing.

As planned, the fox came out of the bushes. "Ps-s-s-st!" he whispered to the woodcutter. "Have you seen any bears around here? I thought I heard a bear."

"Bears?" said the man. "None that I know of."

"And what do you have in that sack?" the fox asked suspiciously.

"Some logs for my fireplace," said the woodcutter. "These are a little too long, but I can soon break them up. See?" He raised his heavy ax and hit the bear a terrible blow through the sack. *Whack!* One groan and the beast was dead. The woodcutter gave another whack just to make sure.

"Good work!" said the fox. "Now, we must act quickly. I will come to your house tomorrow at sunrise to get my seven hens and a rooster. It's really a very small payment for my clever idea, don't you think? I'll see you in the morning!" and he slipped away into the forest.

Very early the next day there was a knock at the woodcutter's door. "I'm here," said the fox. "Let me in. I came to get my chickens, as you promised me. Seven hens and a rooster. Young and healthy." When there was no immediate answer, the fox knocked again, a little louder.

Inside the house the woodcutter began growling and barking and yelping the way foxhounds do when they have been penned up and want to get out. "Be quiet!" he said as he went on barking and making scratching sounds on the door. "Be quiet! I must go see who's at my door so early in the morning. Hush!" and he barked again.

"That sounds like a pack of foxhounds!" said the fox in a worried voice. "Do you have foxhounds in there?"

"Only a few," the woodcutter told him, growling and scratching some more. "Six or eight at the most. But don't worry. I'll tell them that you are a very special friend of mine and that you saved my life. I feel sure they won't bother you then." All the time he was talking, he was scuffing his feet along the floor and scratching his fingernails along the back of the door.

"I don't think I trust a pack of foxhounds," said the fox.

"Remember, this fox is my very good friend," the woodcutter said, as if he were talking to his dogs. "You must stay back while I go to the door. He has come to get some chickens that I promised him. Stay back!"

"Never mind!" squeaked the fox. "I'm too busy to stop right now. I can get those chickens anytime. Just hold on to those dogs until I'm far away."

The woodcutter watched out of the window as the fox leaped away from the door and raced into the forest as fast as his legs could carry him. "If we use our brains," the man told himself happily, "there's nothing to be afraid of."

The fox never came back. As for the woodcutter, he's still alive and happy somewhere in Hungary, unless he has died in the meantime.

LUDAS MATYI'S GEESE

NEAR the town of Döbrög there lived a poor widow who had twenty geese and a lazy son named Ludas Matyi. Ludas had never been known to lift a finger to help his mother, not even to feed the geese.

One day out of a clear sky he announced that he was going to take the geese to the marketplace in Döbrög and sell them. His mother was delighted. At last the boy was showing some ambition.

"But remember, son, the Baron Dobrogy is an old tyrant," she warned him. "He is a very cruel man. He levies terrible taxes on us poor peasants. When we cannot pay he sends his soldiers, the Hajduk, to take the money from us by force. I hope you will not meet him."

"Ha!" laughed Ludas Matyi. "I am not afraid of that old rascal!"

He set off with the geese, driving them ahead of

him on the road to Döbrög, whistling as he went. When he got to the village, the first person he met was the hated Baron, of course.

"How much do you want for those geese?" the Baron called to Ludas Matyi as the fat creatures waddled along, honking and sticking out their black tongues.

"Three forint," said Ludas.

"I'll give you half of that."

"Never!" replied Ludas Matyi. "For such a price I wouldn't even give you the spirit of my dead father, God rest his soul!" He went on down the street, still whistling.

The Baron signaled to his soldiers. Two of them sprang out and threw young Ludas to the ground. One of them held him down while the other one gave him fifty fearful whacks with a big stick. The Baron watched the beating with great pleasure, clapping his hands in time to the whacks.

When the Hajduk finally let young Ludas up, they seized the twenty geese and ran off with them, laughing and laughing and laughing.

Ludas staggered to his feet, hurting all over and barely able to stand. "Thanks for the payment," he told the Baron. "But I promise you, I shall pay you back three times over! I promise you!"

He stumbled to the shade of a tree and sat down to think things over and decide what to do next. He was ashamed to go home and face his mother. She had

warned him of what might happen, but he had refused to listen. He had lost the geese and had received no payment except a beating, so he had nothing to show for his trip to the village but a mass of bruises. He could not go home.

Ludas Matyi began to wander. He went to foreign lands, learned many languages, worked hard for the first time in his life, and saved his money. In all those years of traveling, he never forgot his promise. He would repay the Baron and his soldiers, the Hajduk, if it took forever.

Finally the day came when Ludas Matyi could go back to Döbrög. He started home with a happy heart, but when he got there everyone had forgotten him because he had been gone for so long. His mother was dead and their little house was in ruins. In place of the old castle of the Baron, there was a big new one, almost completed except for the roof. Ludas looked at the castle and thought to himself, "Today I shall begin repaying the Baron!"

He went off to get some clothes that would make him look like an Italian architect—a small black beret for his head, a white silk shirt with flowing sleeves, a handsome pair of dark-green velvet trousers, and a set of pencils to carry in his pocket. He dressed up in the outfit and strolled over to the castle, looking around as if he knew everything there was to know about architecture, pretending to make some notes and sketches, standing back and shading his eyes to get a better view. He made sure that the Baron saw him as he studied the castle. Finally the nobleman approached him.

"My dear sir," he said courteously, "I see that you are an architect. I am greatly in need of someone to help me finish my new castle by putting on a roof. I hope you will be interested in the job. I will pay you well."

Ludas made a pretense of not caring one way or the other since he was so busy, but he finally allowed himself to be persuaded.

"Now," he said to the Baron when they had made their agreement, "if you wish to have a truly beautiful roof, one that will last for generations—and I feel certain that you do as you are known everywhere for your high standards—you must have it made from a very special tree."

"Of course, of course," said the Baron, flattered. "I must always have the best."

"I knew as soon as I saw you and this fine castle that you would never want anything second-rate," Ludas told him.

"How right you are!" said the Baron, even more flattered. "Come with me and I will show you the great forest from which you can select exactly what you need."

Ludas made a big show of looking at the trees and finally found one that he thought might do, but it must be precisely the size that a man's arms could reach around. It must not be either too small or too large.

"Of course!" said the Baron, impressed with the architect's desire for perfection. "To be sure! Here, I'll show you the size of this one." He went to a young oak and put his two arms around the tree, showing Ludas that he could clasp his fingers together.

"Perfect!" said Ludas. "Wonderful!" He reached into his pocket and took out a stout rope. In no time he had tied the Baron's hands together with a tight knot. "Now I have you, you old tyrant!" he shouted. He picked up a heavy stick from the ground and gave the Baron fifty terrible whacks on his back, just as the cruel Hajduk had done to him when they stole the geese. Roaring with laughter, Ludas skipped off into the forest.

When their master did not return, the Baron's servants went to look for him. They finally found him, still tied to the tree and groaning from the pain of the beating, just as Ludas had suffered. They took him home and put him to bed.

Ludas Matyi wasn't satisfied yet. He had promised to repay the Baron three times—this was only the first. He found some plain dark clothes of good quality, painted a moustache on his upper lip, and put on some eyeglasses so that he would look like a doctor.

Carrying a leather bag, which he pretended was full of healing medicines, he went to the Baron's room, telling the servants that he was the physician who had been sent for.

"We found our poor master in the forest," they wailed. "He had been tied to a tree and had been beaten almost to death. We are so glad you have come! But who could have sent for you? We just got home and got our master into bed, just this very minute. Ah, well, do come in! We're so glad you are here."

Clearing his throat and trying to look very learned and solemn, Ludas Matyi went to the bed where the Baron lay moaning and groaning. He took out an immaculate handkerchief and spent several minutes cleaning his glasses, breathing on them, polishing, looking through them to be sure they had no specks of dust on them. The servants watched him with open mouths. Here indeed was a capable man, obviously a fine doctor.

Ludas bent over to examine the Baron's wounds. "Ah-h-h-h-h," he said thoughtfully. He felt the Baron's forehead to see if there was any fever. "Ahemm-m-m-m-m," he said. He leaned down to listen to the Baron's heart. "A very sick man," he said soberly. "A very, very sick man. Now let me see—"

The servants leaped to his side, waiting to be told what to do.

"First," Ludas told them, "I shall need the following herbs." He made up some hard-sounding words from one of the many languages he had learned. "I shall also need—let me see—about two basketfuls of these grasses, which you can probably find in those open fields on the far side of the forest," and he made up

another set of nonsense words. "Get on with it!" he
ordered. "There is not a moment to waste!"

The servants scurried from the room, wondering
if they would be able to remember any of those strange
unpronounceable words, and worrying about what
might happen to them if they came back empty-
handed. The Baron treated his servants as badly as he

treated everyone else, possibly even worse.

"While you are gone, I shall take his pulse," said Ludas Matyi. He lifted one of the Baron's wrists, and by the time the servants were out of the room, he had tied both of the man's hands to the bedpost. Then he told the Baron who he was and proceeded to give him another fifty whacks, while the Baron yelled for mercy. Of course no one could hear him because all the servants had gone on the fool's errand to find herbs and grasses. Ludas Matyi disappeared.

After the Baron had been found beaten twice, there was a great scandal in Döbrög. Everyone was talking about it. Many were delighted, but no one dared to admit it. The mean old tyrant, who was hated by everyone, had finally gotten a dose of his own medicine.

The Baron refused to give up. Now that he knew Ludas Matyi's name, he put a price on Ludas' head. All over the village he nailed up big posters announcing the reward.

It was market day again in Döbrög. Ludas, feeling that he was safe because no one knew what he looked like, went to the stalls where they were selling horses. He saw an especially fine horse being led by a boy.

"How much do you want for this horse?" Ludas asked him.

"One hundred pieces of gold," said the boy.

"Are you crazy?" Ludas frowned. "One hundred pieces of gold! That's too much to pay for one horse."

"It is a very good price," the boy told him. "This is the fastest horse in all the land."

"Prove it!" said Ludas Matyi.

"I'll be glad to," said the boy confidently. "You set the course."

Ludas pointed to the Baron's elaborate coach a little way up the street. "Yonder is a man who has ten soldiers accompanying him," he said. "Ride over there and tell them you are Ludas Matyi. If you can get away from them on that fast horse of yours, I will pay you not only one hundred pieces of gold, as you ask. I will give you one hundred and *ten* pieces of gold. How's that for a bargain?"

"Excellent!" said the boy. He leaped onto the horse and rode toward the ten Hajduk guarding the Baron. When he told them he was Ludas Matyi, they chased him at a furious gallop. While they were gone, Ludas strolled to the coach and gave the Baron fifty terrible whacks. This was the fulfillment of his promise. He had repaid the Baron three times.

Ever since that market day in Döbrög, the Baron has been good and kind, and everyone in the village has been happy.

And if they haven't died, they're still alive.

74

THE FORFEIT

In A LITTLE TOWN of Hungary, during the reign of King Matthias the Just, there lived two men—a young one named Peter and an old one named Istvan.

Even though he was still young, Peter was wealthy because he made and sold wine. In Hungary no man who sells wine is ever poor. Peter had many fine vineyards. In October he always hired men to help him gather the grapes and press them into juice. The fresh juice was then put into large wooden barrels so that it would ferment into wine. In the spring Peter loaded the barrels on his big wagon and went through the countryside selling his wine.

Old Istvan was also rich, richer than Peter, but he was ugly. He was also very stingy. He kept his money locked up in his cellar in a big strong metal chest that was also locked. Old Istvan was the only person who had a key either to the cellar or to the strong metal chest, and he wore the keys on a chain around his neck, out of sight under his clothes.

Surprisingly enough, rich, ugly, stingy old Istvan had a beautiful young wife. He was so jealous of her that he hardly dared let her out of his sight. Sometimes he wished he could lock her up in his cellar too, so that no one but himself could look at her.

One day when Peter came along with his wagonload of wine, Istvan bought many barrels of wine, but he had forgotten to bring any money with him. After all, it was quite a task to unlock his cellar, unlock the big strong metal chest, take out some money, lock the chest, and lock the cellar, so he didn't do it any oftener than he had to.

"Perhaps I can give you a signed paper that says I owe you one thousand gold forint," he said to Peter. "I will promise to pay you before Easter."

"Fine," said Peter. It was not the first time that someone had owed him money, but no one had ever owed him quite so much. A thousand gold forint! But then Istvan was rich—there was no need to worry. And he had promised to pay before Easter.

Time passed. Soon it was Easter. Then it was past Easter. Then it was *way* past Easter. Istvan did not pay Peter the money he owed him. Peter got tired of waiting. Finally he sent his servant to remind Istvan of the debt.

"There was no answer," the servant reported. "All the doors were closed. I knocked and knocked and

yelled and yelled, but no one came."

"We'll try again later," said Peter. But no matter how many times the servant went to Istvan's house or how long he knocked or how loud he yelled, there was no answer. It was as if everyone at Istvan's house had died, and Peter knew that had not happened.

At last he decided to go to a judge. The debt was legal and must be paid. Peter had a signed paper to prove it. One thousand gold forint! The judge listened to his story of what had happened and spent some time studying the paper. After Peter left, the judge put on his hat and walked over to Istvan's house and knocked on the door, a good strong loud knock.

Now Istvan was in a very uncomfortable situation. He did not want to pay the wine merchant the thousand gold forint, but when a judge is knocking on your door, a good strong loud knock, you do not refuse to answer. Especially if the judge has with him four great big policemen with drawn swords, standing right behind him and looking very fierce.

Finally Istvan had to come to the door. He put on his friendliest smile, which made him look like a dried-up old apple.

"What a great honor!" he said graciously. "Do step inside!" He clapped his hands for a servant. "Bring food and drink for our honored guest, His Excellency the Judge!" he ordered. "Quickly!"

Now the judge was human too. He liked very much being called "His Excellency," since he didn't deserve

78

such a title. He was only a small-town judge and not one from the King's Court at all. Istvan noticed that the judge was smiling, which made him look like a dried-up old prune. Nevertheless, the judge did not forget the reason he had come.

"Istvan," he said importantly, "I understand that you owe Peter one thousand gold forint and that you promised to pay him before Easter. It is now well past Easter, and you have never paid him. My good man, my advice to you is that you must pay the debt you owe him within three days or I shall put you in jail. That is the law."

Istvan reached into his moneybag, which he kept strapped around his waist, and took out a gold piece worth ten forint. "You are right, Your Excellency," he said as he held the ten forint in front of the judge's nose. "And I am a man of my word, as everyone knows. I will pay Peter before Easter, just as I have written on the paper. But you will notice, Excellency, that the paper does not specify which Easter. I will pay him before Easter, as I have promised, but no one knows what Easter that will be."

The judge looked at Istvan and at the ten gold forint so close to his nose and at the feast of food and drink that the servant had spread before him. "How right you are, friend Istvan," he said thoughtfully. "How could I have been so blind? I had not noticed that important fact. Thank you for reminding me and for giving me this fine gold piece. Now I believe I would

enjoy eating some of the fine food and drink you have prepared."

The next day Peter rushed over to the judge to hear his decision. He was very much disappointed when the judge told him that Istvan had never said which Easter he meant and that there was nothing that could be done to get his money. The judge was sorry, of course, but it was the law.

The young man decided that he would go straight to the King. When he arrived at the capital city of Buda he went to the palace and asked the guards to let him in. The King was very busy—this was long ago when most kings were busy—so Peter had to wait, but finally he stood in front of the great, beloved Matthias the Just, who was known far and near for his fairness. Peter was so excited that he could not say a word. He just stood there, tongue-tied, staring.

"What can I do for you, my son?" the King asked him kindly, noticing how frightened he was. "Speak up! I won't bite you!" Peter finally came to life and began pouring out the whole story.

"H'm," said the King, walking up and down with his hands behind his back, as he always did when he was thinking hard about something. "H'm. Let me see. H'm." Finally he told Peter to go to an inn and wait for a message from him. The young man thanked the King and bowed out of the palace. He found an inn nearby and settled down to wait.

Meanwhile, one of the King's fastest messengers

was saddling his fastest horse. In his saddlebag was a letter bearing the King's seal and saying:

My dear subject, Istvan:

We have heard many fine things about you and your wealth, and especially about your ability as a merchant. Such a man should surely be here in our great capital city where his many talents can be appreciated. We have also heard that you have an exceedingly beautiful wife. Surely her beauty should not be hidden in such a small country town! She should be one of the jewels of our Court. It is my wish, my dear subject, that you and your wife come to Buda as soon as possible.

(Signed) Matthias Rex
King of Hungary

When rich, ugly, stingy old Istvan received this letter, he hurried around all over town showing it to everyone. "It's a letter from the King!" he told them. "See this seal? That's the King's seal. See where it says 'signed'? That's where the King signed it himself. This is a letter written to me, Istvan! It's a letter from the King! See my name there at the top? He wrote the letter to me!"

He ordered his servants to begin packing immediately. The next day he and his beautiful wife set out for the capital city.

In Buda he showed his letter to the guards, and they sent him right in to the King. "When you have a letter from the King, with his seal on it, you can go anywhere," Istvan told his wife. "Even these guards know that I am a very important fellow."

82

As soon as the pair were inside the courtyard of the palace, one of the guards leaped on his horse and galloped off to Peter's inn to tell him that the old miser and his wife had arrived.

A steward asked Istvan and his wife to wait for a few moments until the King had time to see them— Matthias was a very busy man, as everyone knew. "Yes, of course," said Istvan, trying to smile even though it hurt his face. "We don't mind waiting. Not at all."

In a little while he was told to come to the King's throne. He was a very proud man as he followed the steward, carrying his letter, striding along as if he were the King himself.

Imagine his surprise when he saw Peter standing there, right beside Matthias the Just! The cracked smile on Istvan's face disappeared in an instant. What was Peter doing at the palace? He dared not speak until the King spoke to him, but a thousand questions raced through his mind.

"We are happy to see you," said the King. "But we would be much happier if the circumstances of your visit were different. We have heard complaints that you have not paid your honest debts to this young man. It is well known all over Hungary that you are a rich man. What excuse do you have?"

"But, Your Majesty," said Istvan, bowing so low that he almost lost his balance, "it is not true that I am rich. The real truth is that I am very, very poor. I have hardly enough to eat! You can see how thin I am." He drew in his cheeks until his face was a mass of wrinkles. "Oh, Your Majesty, you must believe me! If I had even one forint to my name, I would pay this fine young man everything I owe him. It is impossible, Your Majesty!"

"Sad," said the King. "Very sad. But it is an honest debt. And since you have no money to pay it, we must command you to give to Peter a forfeit."

"Ah," said Istvan, secretly pleased, "I do not have anything that would be worth a thousand gold forint!"

King Matthias, wise in the ways of people like Istvan, smiled down at him. "Let us decide that," he said. "By the way, where is your wife?"

"She is outside, Your Majesty, waiting for me."

"Call her in," said the King. "I would like to see her, as I have heard so much of her beauty." He signaled to a steward, who went to bring Istvan's wife into the room. The King was amazed. She was just as beautiful as everyone said she was! No wonder Istvan was so jealous!

"You say you have nothing that is worth one thousand gold forint?" the King asked Istvan.

"Nothing, Your Majesty. I am a poor man. Desperately poor."

"Sad," said His Majesty, as he motioned to Peter. "Come here, young man. You may keep this beautiful lady until her husband, who is desperately poor, can somehow find the money to pay you what he owes you.

She will be his forfeit until he can pay his honest debt. The matter is closed."

The King got up from his throne and left the room.

Young Peter reached out to take the beautiful lady with him. In an instant, Istvan put one thousand gold forint into Peter's outstretched hand and the debt was paid, all in shining gold pieces.

THE BEST OF
THE WORST

ORDINARILY King Matthias the Just was a happy man, but now he was bored. Nothing interested him. Not the court fool, who could make the gloomiest old monks laugh. Not the court wizards, who could predict the future and were always telling him of exciting things that were going to happen. Not even his brave knights, who were putting on a show in front of the palace. Nothing could rouse the King.

Finally the Captain of the royal guard could not stand it any longer. "Your Majesty," he said, "I want to do something to cheer you up. No matter how much it costs or how difficult it is to find, you must have whatever you want. Make a wish! If it is humanly possible, I shall get it for you. Make a wish!"

The King sat with his head in his hands. At last he said, "My kingdom has the best of everything—gold, jewels, palaces, soldiers, wizards, minstrels, magicians,

even the best cooks, and the best gardeners. Isn't that right?"

"Yes, Your Majesty, the best," said the Captain anxiously. "What is missing?"

"The lazy people!" said the King. "We have the best of the people who work hard and make us proud of them, but we've forgotten the lazy ones. We must have the best of those too."

"But of course!" said the Captain, greatly relieved. "Only Your Majesty would have remembered the laziest ones!" Clapping his hands to summon the royal guards, he hurried from the palace, muttering to himself, "Now why couldn't I have thought of that?"

Beginning to cheer up immediately, the King sent for the royal carpenters and ordered them to build a beautiful cottage in the royal park, to be ready for the newcomers. He had told the Captain to bring him three of the laziest men, so the cottage must have three bedrooms.

The Captain sent his heralds riding throughout the land, sounding great golden trumpets and announcing, "In the name of His Imperial Majesty, Matthias the Just, King of Hungary! Hear ye! Hear ye! Who is the laziest man among you? Have him report to us, the King's heralds, at once. He will not regret it, we promise. Hear ye! In the name of His Majesty, come forth!"

Their task was not going to be easy. In the first place, most of the lazy people were too lazy to listen to the trumpeters and their announcements. Those who heard it accidentally were too lazy to report. The ones who did come were dragged there by their wives, too lazy to resist.

If the King had known how many lazy people there were in his kingdom, he would have been amazed. There were as many lazy people as there were sands in the sea or leaves in the forest. It was hard to believe! The truth was that the lazy ones never left their cozy firesides so that anyone might see them. They sat and smoked their long pipes day and night, stopping only to eat whatever was brought to them. The hard workers had to work twice as hard, just to take care of the burden of the lazy ones.

How could the heralds ever choose only three out of all those hundreds? They soon realized what a difficult mission they had.

In a mountain village they found two men who were father and son. The father had only one leg, because he had been too lazy to defend himself when a wolf attacked him in the forest. He was so lazy that when his son was born he could not bother to think up a name, so the boy was called "That."

Young That was even lazier than his father, since he would not eat unless he was fed. He was almost seven feet tall and grossly fat, so he must have found someone to feed him. Finally the heralds chose him instead of his father.

"He *looks* so lazy," they said judiciously. "The King will be pleased."

Because of That's great weight, the heralds harnessed two horses together and put him across them. All the people in the village had to help get him in place. When they rode away with That fastened securely across the horses' backs, his father was too lazy to lift his hand and wave good-by.

"Perhaps we chose the wrong one!" said a worried herald. "Perhaps we should have taken his father instead!"

"Never look back!" his companion told him firmly. "That is lazy enough. We aren't making a mistake."

At a country crossroads they selected another candidate, a man so lazy that his eyes were always open. He was too lazy to blink. Because his eyes were round and bright and he seemed to see everything, many did not notice his laziness, and he was too lazy to explain. The heralds' spirits began to rise.

"It's getting easier, isn't it?" asked one.

"It's fun," said another. "I'm enjoying this."

But finding the third lazy one was not so easy, because they had so many to choose from. After a long discussion they decided on a funny little man with hair falling to his ankles over a beard just as long. He sat all day, every day, in the village square. Many strangers thought he was a local monument.

Pigeons clustered and fluttered around him. He stayed alive by catching scraps of food that passersby threw to the birds but which fell on him instead. His long hair and beard kept him warm in the winter, like a heavy blanket. When summer came, he moved several feet away to the shade of a tree to get out of the sun.

"This is the man!" the heralds agreed. "The King will surely reward us for doing our work so well. Three lazy men already! The best of the worst!"

By the time the heralds and the men reached the capital city of Buda, the new cottage was ready for them. It glittered with splendid furniture, carpets, lamps, and paintings. The fireplace was big enough to burn a whole tree. Satin pillows were placed at every possible spot where the men might wish to rest. Handsome long pipes and expensive tobaccos were laid out on low trays waiting to be smoked. Music played throughout the house and long tables held platters of delicious food. Vases of pretty flowers stood in every room.

The King stood waiting to greet the three men with servants, cooks, and pages lined up behind him. He rushed to embrace the three as the heralds got them down from the horses and half carried them to the house, since they were all too lazy to walk. When That rolled off the two horses to the ground, he made a great thump like the sound of thunder, but he was too fat to notice the jolt.

Soon the three were settled down to a comfortable life of doing nothing but eating, drinking, and smoking. The servants filled their pipes and lighted them, fed them their food, poured rare wines into golden

goblets and held them to the lazy men's lips. The King visited the men faithfully every morning, but everyone else soon forgot all about them.

One morning when King Matthias had just left and the servants had carried away the dishes to be washed, the three were lolling on their satin cushions when That said in a rumbling voice, "Something is burning."

After a long while the man who never closed his eyes slid farther down on his cushion and reported that the room was full of smoke.

After another long while the Monument growled, "You talk too much."

By the time anyone else noticed the smoke, it was too late. The new cottage with its elegant furniture, its fireplace big enough for a whole tree, and its tables of delicious food, had burned to the ground. The three men were too lazy to put out the fire.

There was nothing left but a big empty place in the middle of the royal park, the most beautiful park in all of Hungary.

THE PRINCE
WITH THE
TERRIBLE TEMPER

ONCE there was a prince who would someday be
the King of Hungary. He was strong, brave, honorable,
thoughtful, and just. He was a fine horseman and
could handle a sword with great skill. He would make
a good king for his people except for one thing—his
terrible temper. If something went wrong or he got
upset, he could explode like a rocket and frighten
everyone around him.

"Of course he's still young," the old men assured
those who worried about his lack of self-control. "Give
him time." But still some of them shook their heads.
Such a temper was bound to get the prince into
trouble sooner or later. And was there any way it
could be put to good use? They thought not.

One day the prince and his friends were romping
in the park, running and jumping and hiding from
each other, laughing and shouting. Without realizing

what he had done, the prince accidentally pushed down an old lady who was gathering twigs for a cooking fire. He went racing off to the far end of the park, daring his friends to catch him, unaware of what had happened.

The old woman, who was really a witch in disguise, brushed off her clothes and made sure that none of her bones were broken. Then she raised her scrawny hand and put a curse on the boy, to punish him for his rudeness.

"*Dirom-durom-darom!*" she said darkly, using the most powerful words she knew. "*Dirom-durom-darom! May the first wish that you say out loud come true!*" Muttering to herself, she made a mysterious sign with her bony fingers and disappeared into the forest.

If only the prince had known about the witch's curse, he could have wished for something fine, and he would have received it, but that was not to be. He went scampering home, and when he got back to the palace he found his three sisters tossing balls back and forth to each other. To tease their brother, who was the youngest in the family, they threw the balls at him.

Whoosh! Just like that his temper flashed out. "I wish that every one of you would disappear from the face of the earth!" he screeched.

And they did. The places where the three princesses had been standing were all empty. There was no sign of them anywhere. The prince was alarmed. What had happened? Had he been dreaming? Hadn't his

sisters been right there in the courtyard only an instant ago? He looked everywhere, in all the hiding places he knew, in doorways, in the tree branches, behind the shrubs. There was no one anywhere near. Finally, being an honorable fellow, he went to tell his father what had happened.

"My beautiful daughters!" cried the King. "We must find them! What could have become of them? My darling little princesses! All gone!"

"Even if I have to search every corner of the world, I will find them, Father," the prince consoled him. "I will have the smith make me a pair of iron shoes and ask the armorer to make me the finest sword in Hungary. Then I shall set out to look for them. I will never stop looking for them until the iron shoes wear out or the sword is rusted to nothing."

His parents were weeping bitterly when the prince left home to hunt for his sisters, so he hurried away as fast as he could. He walked and walked, day after day, stopped everyone he met to ask if they had seen the three princesses or knew anything about them. No one could help him.

After many discouraging days he came to a crossroads where some young men were having a violent argument. They looked surprised when the prince spoke to them, and for a good reason—the three were not human but were male witches, called warlocks. People never dared speak to them.

"What are you quarreling about?" the prince asked

them, having no way of knowing who they were.

"When our father died," the oldest one replied, "he left us three things, to be divided among us—a cap, a purse, and a pair of boots."

"Is that all you are fighting over?" the prince asked them, puzzled.

"These are not ordinary things," the warlock explained. "The cap will make you invisible, the purse is never out of money, and the boots will take you anyplace you want to go. Instantly! So each of us wants all of them."

"Naturally," the prince told them. "Well, perhaps I can help you. When I count to three, all of you start running to that hilltop just beyond the pine trees. The first one to reach the top and get back here will win all three of the treasures. Fair enough?"

"Fine!" the warlocks agreed, so the prince began counting. "One! Two! Three!" and off they went.

As soon as their backs were turned, the prince put on the cap, pulled the magic boots over his own, and slipped the purse into his pocket. When the warlocks came running back from their race, he was nowhere to be seen because the cap had made him invisible.

"Where are you, you big cheater?" the warlocks shrieked to the thin air. "We'll get even with you, you terrible crook! We'll show you what tempers we have when someone makes us angry!" They waved their arms around everywhere, hoping to hit him and knock him down.

Looking down at the boots, the prince whispered, "I wish that you might take me to the ends of the earth!" And they did, instantly, as the warlocks had promised.

But getting to the ends of the earth was no help, because he found no sign of his sisters even there, and he had been everywhere else. The prince sat on the edge of the earth, dangling his feet into space, his young face troubled. "What am I to do now?" he asked himself bitterly. "I have come clear to the ends of the earth and I still have not found my beautiful sisters." He wanted to cry, but a brave prince never does that, so he asked himself another question. "Is there anyone who can see everything that goes on in the whole world?"

Like a flash came the answer—the Sun! "Magic boots," he asked them, "please take me to the house of the Sun." And they did.

The Sun was not yet home from his daily trip around the world, but his mother greeted the prince kindly and said she would help him. When it got dark the Sun came in, crimson with anger. "I smell a human, an earthling!" he roared. The prince began to quiver. What a temper the Sun had! "A human is here! Where is he? I must find him so I can burn him to ashes!" The Sun blew out great puffs of smoke and flame.

"Please quiet down," the Sun's mother begged. "This young man is our guest. You must always be

courteous to people who come to your home, whether you like them or not. You should know that."

"I'm sorry," said the Sun, beginning to simmer down. "Now, young fellow, what is your story?"

The prince choked out a few frightened words, trying to tell the Sun about his sisters, but the Sun knew nothing about them. "However," he said thoughtfully, "I work only in the daytime. Perhaps my sister, the Moon, who takes over at night, may be able to help you. I shall give you this golden hair from my head so that she will believe you when you tell her I have sent you. She is apt to be a bit suspicious, you know."

The prince thanked him, and, taking the golden hair carefully between his fingers, he asked the magic boots to take him to the Moon. She was more polite than the Sun, but still she treated the prince coolly and said she had no idea where the princesses might be.

"I suspect," she told him, "that some witch has put a curse on them. Or perhaps on you."

"But why?" the prince asked, dumbfounded. "Why?"

"You'll have to figure that out for yourself," the Moon told him. "Perhaps my uncle, the Wind, may know something, because he gets into places that neither the Sun nor I can reach. Tell him I sent you."

The Wind received the boy with great friendliness. "I may know where your sisters are," he told him breezily. "But it is a long and dangerous journey. Do you think you want to try it?"

"Of course! My sisters are very precious to me. And I have magic boots that will take me anywhere, a cap that makes me invisible, and a purse that is never out of money."

"How did you get them?" the Wind asked him.

"I borrowed them," said the prince. "I'll return them when I find the princesses."

"You're lucky," the Wind whistled enviously. "But I warn you that your treasures will lose their magic power as soon as you come to the glass mountain, which is controlled by a certain old witch. You must climb that mountain all by yourself. On the other side of it is a golden forest. You must walk through that forest without touching a leaf until you come to a clearing. In the middle of the clearing you will see a fine castle, but it won't be like any castle you have ever seen. It will be sitting on an island shaped like a duck's foot and it will be turning around like a top."

"Yes? And then?" the prince asked breathlessly.

"Your sisters are in that castle, my boy. They have not been harmed, but they cannot get out unless you rescue them."

"I must go to them at once!" said the prince, rushing off. In no time the boots took him to the foot of the glass mountain, but when he stopped to look up at the great, shining cliffs he heard a clanking sound as his iron shoes kicked against a stone. The noise sounded something like *dirom-durom-darom*. He glanced down at his feet. The magic boots were gone!

He felt in his pockets. He had no money, not even a purse! All he had was his wonderful sword, the finest sword in Hungary, and his heavy iron shoes, which would wear forever.

Startled, he stepped back a little and saw his own reflection in the glass mountain, as clearly as though he were looking in a mirror. He was no longer invisible, that was certain! Far in the distance he could see the three warlocks going off with the boots, the cap, and the purse, still quarreling.

"Well, at least they won't hinder me," he thought with relief. "But they won't help me either, come to think of it. Do I have anyone to help me? Oh, how did I get into this awful situation? And how shall I get out of it and save my beautiful sisters, the three princesses?"

??

What did the prince do? How should the story end? A prince who will someday be the king must never give up—everyone knows that. Maybe the Sun, the Moon, and the Wind will help him. And what about that terrible temper? This story has as many different endings as there are people who tell it, so each person who hears it must make up his own ending.

ONLY ONE
DOG MARKET IN BUDA

"THERE WAS only one dog market in Buda!" This is a familiar saying in Hungary. It means somewhat the same as a phrase that is common in America: "Lightning never strikes twice." Here is the way the Hungarian saying got its start.

In the springtime after the snow was gone and it was time to plant the fields, King Matthias the Just liked to walk through the countryside to watch his people working on their farms.

One day he noticed a man plowing with two oxen hitched to a yoke in front of the plow. Only a few acres away another man was plowing, but he had six oxen. This second man was going much faster and getting much more work done than the first one, so the King went over to him and asked, "My good fellow, why not lend your neighbor two of your oxen? That way each of you would have four oxen to pull your plows and he could work as fast as you do."

"Your Majesty," said the man, frowning, "I am surprised that you cannot see that he is a poor man and I am a rich man. Why should I give him any of my possessions, or even lend him two of my oxen? Let him get his own."

"Oh," said the King thoughtfully. "So that's the way it is."

He turned away and walked to where the first man was guiding his heavy plow behind his two beasts. "Come here, please," he called to the man. "I want to give you some advice. You are to sell your two oxen and with the money you receive for them you are to buy all the dogs you can find."

"Sell my animals and buy dogs, Your Majesty?" The poor fellow wasn't sure that he had heard correctly.

"Yes," said the King. "And when you have purchased the dogs, bring them to me at my capital in the city of Buda. You will not regret this, I promise you." He smiled mysteriously at the farmer and continued on his walk through the countryside.

Knowing that the King was always wise and honest, the poor man did as he had been told, although he could not understand the reason. Soon he arrived in Buda with a noisy pack of dogs—little dogs, big dogs, ugly dogs, pretty dogs, black, brown, yellow, white, spotted, dotted, old, young, fat, thin—all of them barking because they were so excited about their trip to the big city. What a yapping they made as the farmer herded them through the streets! Everyone for miles around wondered what was going on.

The guards soon ushered the man into the King's palace. Matthias the Just greeted him and told him that he would buy all the dogs. He paid the farmer an unbelievably large sum of money. Never in the whole world had anyone paid so much for dogs! A fortune, no less!

Suddenly the poor man had become a rich man!

Even before the man got back to his home, there was much gossiping about his new wealth. The news had traveled faster than the wind, faster even than lightning. And of course the rich man who was his neighbor heard about it at once. He hurried off that instant to sell his six oxen and buy dogs with the money. He would have three times the amount of money the poor man had received for his oxen, so he could buy three times as many dogs!

In a few days the rich man entered the capital city in the midst of an enormous pack of dogs, three times as many as the first man had brought. And at least three times as noisy. Maybe five times! No one in all of Hungary had ever heard such yelping!

Stumbling over some of the bigger dogs, who were the size of his oxen and who seemed to be every place at once, the man went up to the palace guards. "I must see the King," he told them importantly. "I am bringing dogs to sell to the King. Let me past!"

At that moment the King himself appeared.

"Your Majesty!" the rich man saluted him with a formal bow and a great flourish of his hat. "I understand that you want to buy some dogs. I have brought you a fine supply."

"*I know!*" said the King, putting his hands to his ears and trying to make himself heard over the uproar. "Get them out of here! This instant!"

"But I thought—" stammered the farmer as a powerful mastiff nearly knocked him over.

"Go home!" shouted the King. "And take all those brutes with you. Guards, get that mob out of here. Immediately!"

"But I thought—" the farmer said again.

"*Out!*" ordered the King. "*There was only one dog market in Buda.*"

THE SHACKLES
AT KÖHALOM

THERE was once a brave and handsome man
named Károly, who had been knighted by the King.
During one of the wars that the Hungarians were
always having with their old enemies the Turks, the
knight Károly was captured and carried off to the
Turkish capital, Constantinople. There he was put
in the Seven Towers in chains. The prison, called
Jedikula in Turkish, was the strongest in the world.
No one had ever escaped from it. Many hundreds of
men had died there.

As was the custom in those days, the Turks sent
word to the wife of the knight that he was locked up
in the Seven Towers and that she could obtain his release by sending them a large sum of money. The
knight was rich, so every day he expected that the
money would come to pay for his freedom. He sat in
the dank, gloomy prison day after day, thinking always

of his beautiful children and of how much they must be missing him. They must surely be eager for his safe return to Köhalom. He could almost hear their voices, calling to him to hurry home. Sometimes the sounds were so real that he sat with his hands over his ears to shut them out.

Weeks went by. The money did not arrive. The Turks sent a more urgent message to the wife of the knight. They knew that she could easily get whatever sum of money they asked for, and they would much rather have the money than the knight. She did not reply.

Károly sat in his chains, despondent and sad. Every night and every morning he prayed for his release. The days were all the same. He always began the morning with an agonized prayer for the arrival of the ransom money. The minutes and hours dragged wearily along as he waited for news. By evening he was sadder than ever. The heavy shackles seemed about to break his bones as well as his spirit. Still he prayed, fervently and devoutly.

One of his fellow prisoners was a fierce foot soldier, a Blue Darabant. He watched the knight's constant praying with a cynical look in his eyes. "Why are you saying those prayers, my man?" he would growl, rattling his chains.

"So that God may free me, of course," answered the knight.

"Has he freed you yet?"

"No, you can see that."

"But still you keep on praying!" the Blue Darabant mocked him. "Either you are a very stupid man, or you are praying to a God who doesn't hear you and doesn't care for you!"

"You are a blasphemer!" said the knight. "You take the name of God in vain!"

"Oh, no, I don't!" retorted the foot soldier. "You do! Because I know who the true God is."

"You are a blasphemer!" repeated the knight in a shocked whisper.

"No, I am a warlock, an angel of the Devil," said the Blue Darabant, his wicked eyes glittering. "The women in our organization, who are usually better known, are called witches. I'm sure you've heard of us?"

The knight nodded, horrified.

"You may go on praying to your God as long as you want to, of course," said the warlock, laughing. "That's your privilege. But I can assure you that it will not do one particle of good. Your prayers are not being heard and they will not be answered. You will lie right here in those shackles and rot, as have countless men before you." His hideous laughter echoed through the dungeon, and he rattled his chains some more, making the knight shudder.

The next morning Károly resumed his prayers, fearing that God might strike him dead for even listening to the warlock. He prayed faithfully morning and eve-

ning—sometimes at noon. There was only silence and the steady taunting of the warlock, telling him that his prayers were useless.

Finally the knight gave up. Completely discouraged, he turned to the Blue Darabant and said bitterly, "You win. Teach me how to pray to your God, who must be the only true one. I have no other hope of ever getting out of this horrible dungeon and returning to my children and my castle at Köhalom."

"At last!" said the warlock, with an evil grin. "You are beginning to show some sense. Now, here is the way you are to begin." Instead of kneeling with his head bowed, as the knight had been doing, the warlock stretched out full length on the board that was supposed to be his bed, keeping his eyes wide open. When the knight had done the same, the warlock told him, "You are to repeat after me these words: 'Our Father, who art in Hell . . .' "

Károly gasped. The Blue Darabant rattled his chains. "Say it!"

"Our F-father, wh-wh-who art in—in—in—" the knight mumbled.

"Louder! Clearer!"

Károly was half strangled, but he began again. "Our F-father—"

"That's a little better," said the warlock. "You must do it seven times. Seven is always a magic number."

There is no magic in the Seven Towers, the knight thought sadly, as he choked out the sinful words.

When they had said the prayer the seventh time, the warlock unsnapped his own shackles with no trouble at all, reached for his big blue cloak, and spread it out on the floor. "Now, my gentleman," he said to the quivering knight, "you must hold tight to my cloak. You must keep your eyes tightly closed. You dare not open them until I tell you to, under pain of instant death. *Do you understand?*"

Károly nodded, too frightened to speak.

"Ready?" The Blue Darabant's snaggled teeth showed in a fiendish grin. "I do love to go on trips. Remember, you must obey my orders exactly."

Károly shut his eyes and took a firm hold on the big blue cloak, thinking only of his home and children. After all, he told himself, he had nothing to lose. And everything to gain!

Suddenly his shackles were loose from the wall! He hardly dared believe it. The cloak began to rise, steadily and gracefully. Like magic the two men floated out through the heavily barred windows. The knight could smell the freshness of the air and hear the sounds of people and animals as he and the warlock flew away from Jedikula, but he dared not look to see the route they were taking. All that mattered was that they were on their way.

"Now!" said the warlock. "You may open your eyes. This is Köhalom!" He took the knight's iron shackles and fastened them to the wall as Károly got to his feet and cautiously opened one eye, fearful that he had been betrayed. But it was Köhalom! It was his own castle, and he was home! He opened the other eye and began to walk excitedly around the courtyard.

"But where are my children, my beautiful children?" he asked. "I don't even hear their voices. They were always playing and making a lot of noise. Where are my little ones?" he begged of the empty air.

Then he saw a row of small coffins lined up by the castle gate. Several larger coffins sat near them. "Are those—are those my children?" he wept. "And the larger ones?"

"Your sisters," said the warlock, cackling with pleasure. "All the members of your family are dead except your wife."

"My wife? My wife, who wouldn't even send money to ransom me from the Seven Towers?" The knight threw himself violently across the row of coffins, weeping inconsolably.

"Why are you crying?" asked the warlock with a sneer. "What did you expect? You turned to the Devil and acted as if he were your God. Naturally God would turn against you and take back what is His own. Why weep? You should have been wise enough to know what might happen."

"But—but you promised!"

"Oh, no, I didn't. I *suggested*," the warlock reminded him. "And you accepted. Let's keep the record straight, my gentleman."

"But—but why was my wife spared, if all my lovely

children were taken from me?" asked the heartbroken knight. "Why not my wife, who is so cruel that she would not ransom me from prison?"

"Your wife is one of us," the warlock told him gleefully. "Surely you must have known that? Or at least suspected it?"

Finally the knight, who had learned a frightful lesson, built a beautiful chapel in praise to God so that the Devil might be angry with him and come to carry off his wife, but even the Devil didn't want her. And if she hasn't died, she's four hundred years old now.

And the shackles? Long after the knight died, his beautiful Köhalom fell into the hands of men as cruel as his wife had been. They made it a prison and used the very shackles that had imprisoned Károly to chain their prisoners to the wall. And the warlock, the angel of the Devil, watched them with delight.

Köhalom is so strong and so well fortified that it has been able to withstand many heavy sieges. Even as long as six hundred years ago the powerful King Michael of Romania failed to conquer it. Still visible on one of its ancient stone walls are the words carved three hundred years ago by a captive who used the long days and nights to chip them out, perhaps with only his fingernails as tools. This is their message: "I, András Bánfi, was here since 1678."

Did he die there? Was he ever released? What kind

of crime had he committed? No one knows, or ever will. But the iron shackles that chained him so cruelly to the wall—they were the shackles of a brave and handsome knight named Károly.

And those who know the castle know that all of this is true.

THE TWO FISHERMEN

ONCE there were two brothers who lived near a lake. One of them was very poor and the other very rich. The poor one tried to make a living for his many children by fishing in the lake, but no matter how long or how hard he worked, he could never earn enough to take care of his big family. The rich brother lived all alone in a fine house on a hill and was very selfish and miserly.

In the middle of the lake there was a water sprite who knew how hard the poor fisherman struggled to try to support his family. On a certain morning the water sprite decided to surprise the man by putting a valuable diamond in the bottom of his net. When the fisherman had hauled in the net and taken out the few fish it held, he noticed something sparkling on the ground. He picked it up and studied it, turning it over and over in his hand. He had no idea what it was or what he should do with it, so he decided to take it to the King.

The King was very happy to know that he had such an honest man in his kingdom. He rewarded the fisherman with many beautiful gifts as well as a large sum of money for bringing him the diamond. Overjoyed with his good fortune, the man hurried home with his treasures and put them in a big pile in the center of the floor. He called his family to come and see what he had brought them.

His wife could hardly believe her eyes. He had to convince her that the King had actually given him all the valuable gifts and that the money was real. She had never seen so much money all at once.

"You must count it," she said, being a very practical person. "We must know exactly how much money we have. My husband," she asked for the dozenth time, "are you truly sure that this money is real?"

"It is real," he assured her. "But when we get it counted, what can we put it in? We don't have a box or a kettle or a sack or anything large enough to hold so much."

"We need a basket," she decided. "A great big one." Then, because her youngest son could run the fastest of all her children, she sent him to the house where her husband's rich brother lived. The boy raced up the hill.

"What are you going to do with such a big basket?" asked the rich brother as he scowled down at the little

boy. He hardly recognized the child as his own nephew because he never paid any attention to the family.

"We are going to count our money," the boy told him. "Thank you for letting us use this." He hurried toward his home with the borrowed basket, which was almost as big as he was.

"Count their *money?*" the rich man mused as he

watched the youngster slipping and sliding down the hill. "They don't have anything! I'll wager they don't always get enough to eat. How can they talk about counting money? I must have misunderstood the child. He's really a ragamuffin, they're so poor. *Money,* did he say?" Finally he could stand it no longer. Secretly, he slipped out of his big house and followed the little boy down the hill, being careful that no one saw him or heard him.

Outside the window of his brother's cottage he hid himself behind some bushes so that he could peek in. Sure enough, the whole family was gathered in the middle of the room counting out, piece by piece, a big stack of gold and silver coins that lay on the floor. Each counted piece was dropped into the basket.

"One thousand and eighty-nine—one thousand and ninety . . ." He could hear the biggest boy repeating the numbers after his father. "One thousand and ninety-one—one thousand and . . ." After each number there was a small *clank!* as the coin fell on others in the basket. "One thousand and ninety-three, *clank!* —one thousand and ninety-four, *clank!*—one . . ."

Furious, the rich man stormed into the house, forgetting that he had been hiding. "Where did you get all that?" he raged, waving his arms and looking very fierce. "You must have stolen it! Everyone knows that you do not earn enough to take care of this big brood of children, let alone having extra money to count! You are a thief!"

126

His brother didn't bother to look up. "I am not a thief," he said calmly, as he went on counting. "One thousand and ninety-five, *clank!*—I found a beautiful jewel in my fishing net—one thousand and ninety-six, *clank!*—and the King gave me this wonderful reward for being so honest and for taking it to him. One thous—"

"Hmph!" snorted the rich brother. "Maybe I should try fishing in the lake myself! Maybe I'll catch a beautiful jewel too!"

"Go ahead," said the fisherman, still counting. "Plenty of fish that have never been caught, you know. One thousand and—"

"That's exactly what I'm going to do! Right this minute!" He rushed from the house, picking up one of his brother's nets as he ran to the water's edge. "That's just what I'll do! Who does he think he is?"

He threw the net into the lake, pulled it out, threw it in, pulled it out, not realizing that he could never catch anything that way, even if the lake were swarming with fish. He didn't give any of them a chance to swim into his net or even to get near it. In! Out! In! Out! He grew crosser and crosser. For nearly two hours he fished as hard and as fast as he could, but he never pulled in anything but water.

Swish! He would throw the net as far as he could. As soon as it touched the water, *swish!* he would pull it up, empty. *Swish! Swish!* He was becoming very angry.

Far in the middle of the lake, out of sight, the water sprite had been watching him and enjoying the sight very much, because he knew how mean and thoughtless and selfish the man was.

Finally, the rich man decided that he might have better luck if he pretended to be his poor brother, so he began to wail, "I'll never catch anything! I've been throwing my net in this lake for half a day and I have not caught one fish. My poor little children will all starve unless I bring them some food!" He tossed the net wildly toward the water, snatching it up again just as before. "I must not let my precious darling children *starve!*"

If he thought he could fool the water sprite with all this loud talk, he was badly mistaken. *Precious darling children,* indeed! The old miser had none of his own and paid no attention to those of his brother.

The water sprite let him fret and fume for a while longer, then he slipped a glittering but worthless stone into the net as it swished near the water. When the man pulled up the net, something shiny fell out.

He was so excited that he could hardly breathe. He picked up the stone, stuck it into a bag, and went racing off to give it to the King.

The guards at the palace gate tried to stop him, but he pushed them away as if they were gnats that were bothering him. "Stand aside, you!" he ordered rudely. "I am bringing a valuable gift for our great King! Out of my way!" Slamming doors and skidding around corners, he ran to the King's throne, shouting, "Your Majesty! Your Majesty!"

"Well, my good man," said the King in some surprise, "what do you have for me that makes you so impatient? It must be something magnificent."

"It is, Your Majesty!" said the rich man, trying to catch his breath and thinking greedily of the fun he was going to have counting his money. "It is truly magnificent. Just wait until you see it!"

He knelt before the King's throne. With a grand gesture he threw open the top of the sack to take out the precious jewel and present it. This was the moment he had been waiting for. His face was wreathed in smiles.

"My gift!" he said with a low, swooping bow. "Just for you, my King!"

Instead of a diamond, or even a precious stone, from the sack there came all kinds of snakes, eels, frogs, worms, spiders, water dwarfs, and every kind of creeping, slimy creature imaginable. They crawled and slithered and hopped and climbed all over the King's beautiful palace. People screamed and screeched and ran in every direction to get away from them. Servants got up on chairs and tables and a few of them tried to jump out the windows. The King stood frozen with disgust.

"So!" he said in a great roar of anger. "So this is the gift you bring me! This is the way you choose to honor your sovereign!" He motioned for his bodyguard

to come get the rich man. "When your humble fisher-man brother brought me a gift," he told him furiously, "I gave him something special as a fitting reward. Now I shall do the same for you. Take him away!"

The miserable prisoner tried to explain, but it was of no use. They dragged him to the open courtyard of the palace. There, for every snake, every eel, every frog, every worm, every spider, every water dwarf, and every creeping, slimy creature that he had turned loose in the King's beautiful palace, they gave him a terrible whack on his back.

And ever since that day the poor fisherman's rich brother has been good and kind and thoughtful and loving and generous and unselfish, and he knows every one of his brother's children—by their first names!

Anyone who doubts this story can go look it up for himself.

THE WELL IN THE ROCK

ABOUT four hundred years ago there was a long and terrible war between the Hungarians and the Turks. It was such a cruel war, on both sides, that people still talk about it. Both the Turks and the Hungarians killed their prisoners at once. The only ones who could escape this fate were the men of high rank, those who had titles such as Baron, Count, or Duke among the Hungarians, or Pasha among the Turks.

When a titled man was taken prisoner, word was sent to his family that he could be set free if they would send a large amount of money as ransom. In this way both sides acquired extra wealth, because the prisoners' families were always willing to send money to save them, no matter how great a sacrifice it meant.

In one battle, a particularly heartless Hungarian Baron captured a young Turkish Pasha. In accordance with the custom, he sent a message to the man's family, asking for ransom money. After a time he noticed that the Turk was unusually restless and anxious for the money to come. Every time a messenger arrived with even the most trivial news, the Turk did everything he could to find out if the message had come from his homeland.

"Why are you so impatient to leave my hospitality?" the Hungarian sneered at him. "Don't you like it here at my castle? My wonderful, magnificent, marvelous castle, sitting up here high on this great rock and overlooking such a beautiful valley? Why should you give a moment's thought to getting away from this glorious spot?"

"It is truly a fine place, just as you say," the Pasha told him, hoping to flatter him. "A splendid castle, simply splendid."

"I suppose you have a finer one?" the Baron snapped. "I suppose you live in a palace, a royal palace more gorgeous than that of the King?" He spat on the ground to emphasize his contempt.

"No, not at all," the Pasha answered.

"Probably the territory in your pashalik is larger and richer and more desirable than the land I control?"

"No, not that."

"Then what is it?" bellowed the Hungarian. He grabbed the Turk by the throat, half throttling him. "What's so much better at home than what we have here?"

"My sweetheart," the Turk said in a strangled voice. "She is beautiful. I love her and she loves me. We have planned our wedding."

"Ha! A wedding, is it?" the Hungarian shouted, dropping the poor Turk to the ground and rubbing his hands together, knowing that this gave him new power. "Well, we shall see about that! A wedding! Wonderful news!"

So he moved the prisoner to a cell that had no windows or fresh air, and cut down on his rations of food. The Turk grew more miserable as time went on, and his treatment became worse and worse.

In due time the money came. The Baron brought it to the Turk's cell and waved it triumphantly under his nose. "Your people must think a great deal of you," he said rudely. "They sent all this money—hundreds of forint—just to get you away from my pleasant company." He counted out the ransom, piece by piece, while the Turk was forced to watch, then he stuffed the money into his pockets and went away, locking the door behind him.

The Pasha began to yell. "Where are you going? You have received a huge ransom for me, so you must release me. I am a free man. Let me out of here at once! At once!"

"Why?" asked the Baron innocently. "I might need you."

"Need me? For what? I am a free man, and you must let me go!"

"I've been noticing how powerful you are," said the Baron. "Exactly the kind of muscles I need for an important piece of work I want to have done here at my castle. When that is completed, of course you will be free to go to the beautiful sweetheart who waits for you."

Enraged, the Pasha began to pound against the bars of his cell. "You have been paid a ransom for me, a proper ransom. I'm supposed to be free!"

"You will be," the Baron promised. "In good time. As soon as you have finished digging me a well."

"Dig you a well? That work is always done by slaves!" the proud Turk protested.

The Baron unlocked the cell door. "Come with me and I will show you where to begin," he said, letting the Pasha breathe fresh air for the first time in weeks. "Right here in the center of this courtyard. Your tools are already here, waiting for you."

"This is solid rock!" protested the prisoner. "It is not a place to try to dig a well!"

"The whole mountain is solid rock," grinned the Hungarian. "And I need a well. The place that I need it is right here, in the highest part of the courtyard. You may begin at once. The other Turkish prisoners who are here will be glad to help you, I know."

"But I have been ransomed!" shouted the Pasha. *"I am a free man!"*

The Hungarian reached for the sword that hung at his belt. "We usually kill our prisoners," he said in a quiet conversational tone, "especially when they give us trouble." He made a brutal slash through the air with the sword. It whistled a half inch from the Turk's ear. "The next time I'll come considerably closer," he went on, "and the third time . . ."

The Turk stared at him, knowing full well that if the sword sliced through the air once more, it would touch him, and the third time it could cut off his head. "But no one ever digs a well in solid rock," he tried to reason with his captor. "There is no water there."

Crack! The sword whipped toward him once more. The Hungarian ran his fingers appreciatively along the sharp edge of the blade. He was getting excited over the idea of using it the third time.

So the Turk began chipping at the rock. The other prisoners were brought out and assigned to help at the impossible task. Each day they began work at the first break of dawn. They continued until it was so dark that they could no longer even see each other. They fell on their hard beds to try to sleep. Soon morning came again, and they were back in the courtyard, whacking and chiseling away, while the Baron amused himself by walking up and down, his sword swinging menacingly, his face brutal.

Some of the men died. The Pasha began to think that they were the lucky ones. He became so thin that he could not keep his clothes on without tying a rope around his waist. His hair turned white. He became permanently stooped from bending over for such long hours. His mind grew clouded. Sometimes he had dreams of health and freedom and happiness, surrounded by memories of his beautiful sweetheart and of the plans they had made for their marriage. Was she still waiting for him? Had she ever received word of his cruel fate? Did she believe him dead?

At other times, when he was even more exhausted and disheartened, he could not remember her, or his parents and brothers and sisters, or anything about his faraway home. He thought he must have spent his entire life digging hopelessly in the rock there at the Hungarian's castle.

A year went by. Two years. The men had made a fairly deep hole, but of course there was no sign of water. The Baron taunted them that they were lazy. They were not working hard enough. They were loafing. He began carrying a leather whip along with his sword. Even the sound of his footsteps made them cringe in fear.

There was a small hill of stone chips that they had tossed out from the depths where they were hacking away at the rock. But there was no water, nor any sign of it. Not in solid rock.

More weeks and months passed. Finally, at the end of still another year, when they had dug down more than three hundred feet, there was an amazing trickle of water! The men were too weak and ill to give more than small, squeaking sounds. Water! Ice-cold, clear,

unbelievable water! They couldn't believe their eyes.

The miracle they had prayed for had actually come to pass—the Baron would be forced to release them. He could not possibly hold them any longer. In truth, the few men who still survived, including the Pasha, were old and broken and nearly dead—but they had succeeded! The water was bubbling up, pure and clear! *Water!*

They set out for their distant homes, barely able to move. At the gate of the castle the Pasha said to the cruel Hungarian, "I hope you will be punished for your unspeakable cruelty. I know you will! If not by our god, then by your god!"

The Baron laughed and waved his sword in the air. "Be gone!" he shouted after them. "Now I shall take a drink of the water you have found for me!"

And he ran to the deep, deep well in the highest spot of his stony courtyard. As he reached down to scoop up some of the clear, cool water, he fell in and was drowned.

No one knows anything about the poor Turkish Pasha and his beautiful sweetheart, but if you go to the Baron's castle on top of the mountain of solid rock, you can see the well, still bubbling with fresh, clear water.

ZOLI THE DOCTOR

A VERY SMALL VILLAGE in the mountains of the Mittelgebirg had one special treasure that no other small village in Hungary boasted—its own doctor. Since he had grown up there, everyone had known him from his babyhood and called him by his first name, Zoli. After he came back from studying medicine with the learned doctors in Buda, they called him Doctor Zoli.

Everyone for miles around depended on Doctor Zoli. He wrapped up their broken arms, bandaged their heads when they got into fights, gave them horrible-tasting medicines when their stomachs hurt, stayed with the old ones when they were dying, and spanked the breath of life into the new ones when they were born.

There was always a light burning in Doctor Zoli's little house, because people came to get him night and

day. Few of them bothered to pay him, but he went right on taking care of them and sometimes of their farm animals as well. He patched up oxen, sheep, horses, donkeys, dogs, and even a few cats. Whenever there was trouble of any kind, Doctor Zoli was the first to know and the first to help.

And so it went for about ten years. Then one autumn day a well-dressed stranger asked a peasant at the edge of the village where the doctor lived. The peasant jerked a thumb over his shoulder. "That house," he said. "Where the doorstep is worn so badly by the people coming to get him all the time."

In no time stories were flying around the village that the stranger had come with an offer of a fine job in the city for Doctor Zoli. Word of the doctor's great skill and his tireless hard work had reached there, and a messenger had been sent to find him. They would give him a fine big house with a separate office, all the surgical tools he needed, a horse for riding and another for pulling the closed carriage that he would use when the weather was bad. Since they were city people, there would be no need for treating farm animals. They promised that he would never have to go out at night except for the very worst cases when no one else could save a patient's life.

"He won't be able to turn it down, will he?" the worried villagers asked each other. "His work will be easy. He'll have lots of money. He won't have to ride horseback through the mountains in a thunderstorm, and he can get a night's sleep every night. What can we do?" They fretted and fumed, trying to find a way out for themselves.

Finally Old Bèla, who was the wisest man in the village because he was the oldest, spoke up. "We must give him a fine gift so he won't leave us. We must let him know how important he is to all of us."

"A great idea!" the others agreed enthusiastically. "Wine! Why not give him a whole barrel of our finest wine?"

"I will contribute the barrel, the biggest, strongest oak barrel that I have," said the local wine merchant, knowing that he could afford to be generous because he would sell much more wine. "I will place it in the square tomorrow morning. We must not lose any more time in gathering up this splendid gift for our dear Doctor Zoli."

143

People came from far and near, carrying pitchers, jars, and buckets, staying around to chat with each other about their pleasure in giving the doctor this token of their affection for him. They talked of their illnesses, their broken legs, their smashed heads, and always it was Doctor Zoli who had saved them.

By midafternoon the barrel was full to the brim. The wine merchant needed three men to help him load it onto his big wagon and transport it to the doctor's little house. The mayor, dressed in his best clothes and wearing his eyeglasses, read a little speech that the village schoolteacher had printed out for him.

"Our beloved Doctor Zoli, our friend," he read, as the paper shook in his hands. "We bring you this gift of the finest wine our Heavenly Father has allowed us to make. We want you to stay with us and take care of us. We need you, our dear Doctor Zoli."

The doctor was nearly overcome. He never dreamed that these good people would do something so wonderful for him. He knew the poverty of many of them, but he also knew of the wealth of others. Both rich and poor had contributed. How thoughtful they were!

He forgot the dozens of people who owed him great sums of money and would never pay him. He forgot the many stormy nights when he had been called out to treat someone who wasn't really sick. He forgot all the people who got worse because they wouldn't take his medicines or follow his orders, and who then blamed him for their troubles. He forgot everything

but the villagers' love for him. He even forgot all their injured oxen, sheep, horses, donkeys, dogs, and a few cats.

That night Doctor Zoli's eyes were misty with tears as he pulled a comfortable chair close to his fire, rested his tired feet on a low stool, and lifted his first glass of the wine to let the firelight shine through it.

"A wonderfully clear color!" he smiled. "Unusually so, considering how many different contributors there were. Although," he added doubtfully, "it isn't very red. All our wines are red. Or purple. Or burgundy." He poked up the fire to give more light. Again he held up his glass. "Very strange. A pure white wine. These wonderful people must have sent to some far-off country to get it especially for me." For a moment he was afraid that he was going to cry like a baby, which, of course, no learned doctor ever does.

"I must taste it," he decided. "I'm sure it has a superb flavor." He took a small sip, then a larger one. "How can this be?" he frowned. "This wonderful wine, the best there is, tastes almost like water!"

He went back to the big oak barrel and poured himself a larger glassful. It didn't smell like wine either, now that he thought of it.

"H'm," he murmured as he took a large gulp.

"H'm!" He drank half a glassful.

"*H'm!*" He opened the barrel and tipped it over on the ground.

Because the wine *was* water! All the people who had

146

come from far and near with their pitchers, jugs, and buckets had poured only water into the big oak barrel, thinking no one would find them out. The poor ones said, "The rich ones can afford to give the best of wines. If my small part is only water, no one will know." The rich people said, "Someone is always coming around and begging us to give something to the poor. This is one time when we can get ahead of them and no one will be the wiser. Who would believe that people like us would put in water?" And their pitchers were the largest of all.

If you think you'd like to visit this little village high up in the mountains of the Mittelgebirg, don't bother. It isn't there any more. After Doctor Zoli left, everyone died, rich and poor, one by one.

THE UGLY PRINCE

ONCE there were two kings in neighboring countries and each of them had a child. The daughter of one king was so beautiful that anyone looking at her felt he had looked at the sun itself, she was so dazzling. The other king had a son the same age, but the poor boy was so ugly that anyone looking at him got a headache.

Since he was a prince of the royal blood, in spite of his appearance, his father thought that a marriage with the beautiful princess from the next country would be most desirable. Consequently, on a certain day, the king put on his finest clothes, dressed his ugly son just as elegantly, and went to call on the other king.

The two monarchs were conversing, and the father of the prince was trying to convince the father of the princess that his son was really an excellent choice as a son-in-law, when the girl came into the room. She took one look at the prince and turned pale. "Father!" she gasped. "I wouldn't have that fellow for a boot-black! Even in those rich clothes, he is so ugly!" And she fled from the room.

In that brief glimpse of the princess, even though she was so scornful, the prince fell in love with her. "Without her, my life isn't anything," he thought sadly. "I must figure out a way to have her for my wife, even if she does think I am too ugly even to be a boot-black."

As soon as he got home, the prince sent for the royal goldsmith. "You must make for me three of the most beautiful pieces of jewelry in the whole world," he told him. "And do it quickly."

The goldsmith was the best and fastest worker in seven countries, but he had never worked so hard. When the designs were finished he sent word to the prince, who asked him to come to the palace at once.

As the goldsmith opened the boxes containing the jewelry he had fashioned, everyone exclaimed about his work. Never had they seen such exquisite creations, so perfectly made. First there was a golden apple, round and shining and looking almost real. Then there was a golden hen, surrounded by twelve golden chicks, each with diamonds for eyes. Most enchanting of all was a golden mirror that began singing the moment someone looked into it:

You are lovely. You are fair.
In all the world there's none so rare.

The prince was delighted. He paid the goldsmith twice his price. Then he packed the jewelry carefully into a bag, disguised himself as a traveler, and went to the castle of the other king. There he asked for a job as a servant.

When they had given him a place to sleep, never

dreaming that he was a prince, he put the sack of jewelry under his bed. At night when his work was finished, he took the golden apple into his hands and began turning it over and over and admiring it, making sure that the princess's personal maid was watching. The girl rushed off to tell the princess.

"Your Highness," she said breathlessly, "do you want to see something unbelievably beautiful? If you do, come with me to the servants' quarters."

So the princess went to see the golden apple. "Give it to me," she ordered. "My father will pay you for it. It is so perfectly fashioned that I must have it for my own."

The servant refused. "I wouldn't sell it for money, Your Highness," he told her. "But if you will give me one kiss, it is yours."

The maid caught her breath. A servant talking that way to the princess! But suddenly the princess reached over to kiss the fellow, picked up the golden apple, and swept from the room.

The next evening the servant took out the golden hen with the twelve golden chicks, and of course the same thing happened. The maid hurried to the princess, told her of the golden hen and chicks with diamonds for their eyes, and brought her to see them.

"Give them to me," the princess ordered. "My father will pay you for them. They are so beautiful that I must have them for my own."

"I wouldn't sell them for money, Your Highness,"

the servant told her, as boldly as before. "But if you will give me two kisses, they are yours."

This time the maid was really frightened. Such a way for a servant to act! But the princess—after a little thought and a few pretty blushes, of course—gave the servant two kisses and carried off the golden hen and the twelve chicks with diamonds for their eyes.

So, on the third day, the servant brought out the singing mirror, making sure that the maid heard it singing, "You are lovely. You are fair . . ."

"Your Highness!" she told her mistress excitedly. "You must see this. It is a mirror that sings when you look into it. You must see it! At once!"

This time the servant asked for *three* kisses. The princess hardly listened to him as the mirror kept singing to her:

> You are lovely. You are fair.
> In all the world there's none so rare.
> You are lovely. You are fair . . .

The servant waited, knowing that she could not resist. "You are lovely . . ." the mirror told her. With a smile, she agreed to give the servant what he asked. But as she was kissing him, her father, the king, came in and saw them. He was very, very angry.

"My daughter kissing a servant," he bellowed. "You refuse to marry any of the princes who have come to court you, and then I catch you kissing a lowly servant boy!"

"But, Father—"

"You are to leave this palace at once! This instant!"
he roared, getting angrier by the minute, his face so
red it was almost purple. "I never want to see you
again. You have disgraced me! *Go!*"

The princess knew that she must obey the king.
This was a long time ago, when even the most beautiful of daughters had to do as she was told. So she went
away from the palace where she had been born and

had spent all her life. The servant boy came running along behind her.

"I have been sent away too," he told her sorrowfully. "Neither of us has a place to go—no home, no family, not even anything to eat or wear. But I will take care of you as well as I can."

The beautiful princess was weeping so hard that she could hardly see him, but she followed him along the road and through the forest until they came to an abandoned hovel at the edge of town.

"At least we can keep dry here," he told her. "And I hope you are not afraid of mice and spiders. Now I must go find some kind of work to do so that I can earn money for our food. I have promised to take care of you, you know."

The princess nodded a reply, unable to speak.

"While I am gone," he told her, "you can clean the mud off my shoes. They got very dirty on our long trip here."

The princess looked surprised, but she was too miserable to answer him.

The servant went off, barefoot. As soon as he was out of sight, he raced to his own castle, because of course he was the ugly prince in disguise. He put on his most magnificent clothes, silks and velvets with gold and silver threads and real jewels woven into the fabric. He ordered his state carriage—you know the one I mean, made of pure gold and drawn by eight snow-white chargers with six footmen dressed in crimson. He sat himself in the carriage and went off in all his splendor to the abandoned hovel.

The princess was sitting in the middle of the floor, trying to polish his dirty boots and finding it very hard work, because she had never done anything like that in her whole life. She looked up, dumbfounded.

"Well, my beautiful princess," said the prince, "you can see that I am not too proud to have *you* for *my* bootblack."

"I am so sorry, my prince," she told him humbly.

"And will you marry me?" he asked her.

"Yes, of course, my prince. Today if you wish."

And so they were married, that very day. The wedding celebration went on for two weeks. I know because I was there and brought home a big piece of the wedding cake to prove it.

If you can find it, you can have it.

ABOUT THE AUTHORS

PEGGY HOFFMANN was born in Delaware, Ohio, and for the past nineteen years has lived in Raleigh, North Carolina, where her husband is State Supervisor of Music for the public schools. They have two sons and a daughter.

Mrs. Hoffmann is a graduate of Miami University, Oxford, Ohio, and has done graduate work at the Chicago Theological Seminary (University of Chicago), Akron University, Colorado State College, and North Carolina State University. Her writing career got its start through an AAUW Creative Writing group at Miami University, where her husband was an associate professor. In addition to books of fiction and nonfiction for both young people and adults, she has published fifteen collections of choral and organ music.

Mrs. Hoffmann met Mr. Bíró, the Hungarian artist

who told her these stories and who has designed this book, through his wife, who was her daughter's roommate at the University of Illinois.

GYURI SANDOR BÍRÓ was born in Budapest, Hungary, in 1942. Several members of his family were jailed there during the Stalin era. Mr. Bíró left the country after the tragic revolution in 1956 and completed high school in Innsbruck, Austria. His first cartoon exhibit was held in Innsbruck in 1961.

He continued his studies at the University of Vienna, where he supported himself and paid for his education by working as an actor, factory worker, model, draftsman, professional boxer, and display man. He has done free-lance work for newspapers and magazines. In 1963, while in Vienna, he designed his first theatrical set; he has been a set designer ever since.

Mr. Bíró has traveled extensively in Europe, Turkey, and North Africa. He is married and since 1966 has lived in the United States, where he has been working in regional and summer stock theater, exhibit and interior design, and TV.